Everyday Training
Backyard Dressage

Everyday ✤ Training
Backyard Dressage

Mary Twelveponies

PUBLICATIONS

MILLWOOD, NEW YORK 10546

Everyday Training text copyright © 1980 by Mary Cleveland

Published 1986 by Breakthrough Publications Inc.,
Millwood, NY 10546

1st Edition 1980 by A.S. Barnes and Co., Inc.

Notice To Readers

The procedures and recommendations contained in this book
should be undertaken only with the proper professional
supervision and accordingly publisher takes no responsibility for
the application of the contents of this book including without
limitation procedures, theories, and product recommendations.

Library of Congress Cataloging in Publication Data
Twelveponies, Mary.
   Everyday training.

   1. Horse-training. 2. Dressage. I. Title.
SF287.T97   636.1′08′88   80-36677
ISBN 0-914327-01-1

Printed in the United States of America

02 01 00 99 98   9 8 7 6 5

For Information address:
Breakthrough Publications
310 N. Highland Ave.
Ossining, NY 10562
www.booksonhorses.com

Dedicated to all horses
"In that day shall there be upon the bells of the
horses, HOLINESS UNTO THE LORD. . ."
ZECHARIAH 14:20

A book of this sort can't be done without the help of
friends. God Bless Them.

Foreword

Everyday Training (Backyard Dressage) is probably the most comprehensive and thoughtfully prepared book on training ever written. It took many months to write and illustrate the lessons Mary Twelveponies spent forty-plus years learning.

Everyday Training (Backyard Dressage) should be mandatory reading for every novice horse owner, and studied by the experienced horseman too. The latter, already familiar with the basic concepts and methodology of horse handling, may well learn better ways or find the "traditional" methods are not traditional at all. Mary Twelveponies learned the classic concepts firsthand. *Everyday Training (Backyard Dressage)* passes them to you.

Mary Twelveponies has assumed a monumental challenge with this book: to improve the general level of horsemanship, and to accomplish it through the much-maligned principles of dressage. Not only is dressage feared and misunderstood, but many feel incapable of learning and later applying dressage techniques with their mounts.

But *Everyday Training (Backyard Dressage)* shows just how wrong these beliefs are. Dressage should *not* be feared, and yes, you *can* learn the techniques that will improve your skills.

Better communication with our horses means less confusion for the horse and, eventually, fewer problem horses. It means less suffering for our silent, stoic steeds at the leaden hands of the uneducated.

If but one rider improves his level of horsemanship through Mary Twelveponies' book, the years of effort and sweat in the arena and over the typewriter will have been worthwhile. But all will come away better riders or owners, and marvel in universal appreciation of Mary Twelveponies' unique gift—true understanding of the splendid beast we call the horse.

Mark Thiffault
Managing Editor, *Horse and Horseman*

Contents

PART THREE
BASIC TRAINING

PART FOUR
SPECIALIZATIONS

Everyday Training
Backyard Dressage

Part One
Introduction

Kathy Hansen and Watirah. The good trainer does not just talk to his horse—he also listens.

INTRODUCTION

I was moved to write this book to help all riders, trainers, instructors and students, regardless of their expertise, reach a better understanding of training and riding according to the mental, emotional and physical abilities of each horse. I was greatly moved to help all horses everywhere get relief from the pain they so patiently suffer because of riding and training methods based on custom rather than on who and what the horse actually is. May the good Lord bless you all with greater understanding, better feel, and improved ability to communicate with your horses and listen to their side of the story.

I have ridden and trained horses for a great many years and by many methods, starting with fumble and stumble and progressing through hit and miss, riding stable English, movie western and California reining to dressage. Nowadays a person can go to school to learn horsemanship, but in my day such schools were practically unknown in this country and there were lots of things that women just did not do. My high school principal would not even let

and why.

The interest in this sort of training has been going forward by leaps and bounds (or should I say courbettes and caprioles?) in this country. I think that is great; but like most things, it is also misunderstood. Too many people still get mental pictures of horses doing such things as the Spanish march and rearing. I have even seen dressage articles illustrated with pictures of horses kneeling and bowing their heads. It may be cute for the horse to salute the judge, too, but the judge does not like to see any horse behind the bit even momentarily. Better above than behind.

Others think of dressage in terms of flying changes every stride, canter pirouettes, piaffe and passage. Even a lot of gung-ho purists think in these terms. These beautiful things *are* true dressage, but this level of training is a specialization, as are jumping, reining, barrel racing and park horse, to name a few. A horse trained in these fancy things is a Dressage Horse—a horse trained specifically for dressage competition at national and international levels.

The aim of basic dressage training can be summed up as teaching the horse to go forward willingly under control, straight, relaxed, rhythmic and balanced. When the horse does all these, with reliable acceptance of the bit, he is truly a pleasure horse. He is also ready for schooling in any specialization you care to mention—including dressage.

This is where the enthusiasts in this country fail to get the point across—mostly because they do not really understand it themselves. They say, "Every horse needs dressage," but still turn around and practice dressage by itself, thinking other methods to be sufficient for other purposes. A friend and I tried to get the California Dressage Society to consider writing official tests for "western dressage," thinking to gain more interest in this way. The board tossed it back and forth and finally vetoed it. One member said, "*Western* dressage? How can there possibly be such a thing?" Clothes may make a man, but a saddle does not make a horse. You can put a stock horse through his "routine" with a dressage saddle and a dressage horse through his paces with a stock saddle.

In Combined Training we find a very good proof of our pudding. Those who get high scores in the dressage test go on to get high scores in the other sections—cross-country and stadium jumping. This not only proves the value of this sound basic training, but it also proves that those riders use it in the other sections too. Those who merely practice the test over and over in order to ride it not only do poorly in the test but also in the other sections. A properly trained horse can be ridden quite well through a dressage test without any previous practice of the test, and that is what it is all about—

proper basic training, not learning a routine. This training is to be used in any other type of riding you care to mention.

Certainly you can practice dressage exclusively if that is your thing; but if you prefer to end up with a western or English pleasure horse, games horse, stock horse, gaited horse, jumper or whatever, then you should employ the principles of basic dressage in order to get the very best results. The fact is that originally, proper schooling was practiced here, brought over on the Mayflower or some such ship, but gradually corruptions and imitations crept in. Examples are gypping the horse (dangling him on the end of a line to exercise him), trick gaits of the circus horse, the high head carriage and high action of the gaited horse (artificial results from artificial methods) and the modern reined stock horse which is now so corrupted as to be almost unrecognizable. The original stock horse was trained to stop and turn with all joints of his haunches bent—squatting—but now he bends in the loin, stiff in every joint of his hind legs.

While imitation may be the sincerest flattery, corruption is a sign of laziness. Neither one produces the best results. Better to adopt the real thing than a cheap imitation of it. Better to do a little well than to corrupt the method and hurry through to a corrupted end. But ignorance is a legitimate excuse if knowledge is not available or is so involved as to be discouraging. Many of today's trainers have discovered dressage principles through experimentation. Others stick to insufficient methods because they were taught that way by others before them. If, however, you start from scratch every time, it takes more than a lifetime to get there. If you get misinformation and are bullheaded in sticking with it, a lifetime does not get you anywhere. Better to start with proven knowledge and go forward.

What I want to do is take you step-by-step through this training of the horse, explaining as we go not only how, but why, and what use to make of it. I have found the official language sometimes involved and hard to understand. (What, you may well ask, is the indirect rein of opposition!) Theory is great and necessary, but I have found too much of it can often destroy the rider's feel of the horse. One pupil who studies every minutia of theory he can find remarked, "I may never be the best rider, but I'll be the smartest!" And that is just about where he is yet, although with three of us working on him, he is gradually riding his horse by feel rather than strictly "according to the formula."

I want to act as a translator and simplifier; get this thing down to everyday riding and training, and teach you theory (how you should do it). But I also want to let you know how to feel and apply it. Then when we have gone through the complete training up to the pleasure horse, I want to show you how to apply it to specializations.

EQUIPMENT

Before we get into training the horse, we need to know what equipment we will need. The one piece of equipment that must be right is the bit. If you hurt the horse with the bit, you will never get him relaxed and going forward with lowered head—the first step in correct training. A severe bit combined with unreliable hands ruins a horse faster than anything you care to mention. If he doesn't go forward relaxed with a lowered head, you will never get him trained well for anything.

The only bit to use is the ordinary snaffle. This is the bit with ring cheeks. It can have various types of mouthpieces, but must have some type of ring cheeks—ordinary rings, egg butt or dee rings—in order to be a snaffle. I find this is a very hard point to get across to my students. I show them a snaffle and they have a picture of a snaffle in the text book, but still some of them show up with the so-called western snaffle and even argue with me that it is a snaffle. *No leverage bit is a snaffle regardless of the type*

Snaffle bits: the top one has a flexible rubber bar mouthpiece; the other has a jointed, thick mouthpiece referred to as broken.

The snaffle bridle with the dropped noseband properly placed.

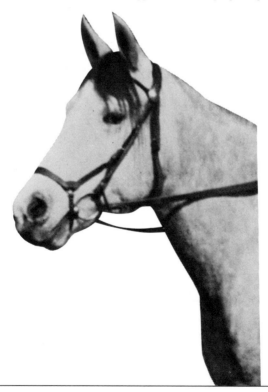

of mouthpiece or if it has no mouthpiece at all. Such a bit is a curb bit.

The best mouthpiece to use is the broken one—one joint in the middle—with the thickest mouthpiece you can find to avoid as much as possible hurting the horse's mouth. Some European snaffles have a mouthpiece three-quarters of an inch in diameter at the thickest part, and this is the most satisfactory thickness. Once in a while you'll run into a horse that is so touchy he needs a rubber mouthpiece. This is a straight bar of flexible rubber and will work for quite a while until the horse accepts the bit. Then you can switch to the regular broken snaffle with the thick mouthpiece.

In order for a horse to be properly trained, he must be taught to bend laterally—bend his spine full length from side to side. The broken snaffle is the most effective tool for this training because you have independent control of each side of the bit. Because the rubber snaffle is flexible, you can get the bend in the horse to a certain extent but not enough for complete training. With a curb bit you cannot get it at all until the horse is thoroughly trained.

The mouthpiece is measured from the inside edges of the rings. A five-inch mouthpiece will fit most horses up to 15.2 hands unless they have exceptionally large muzzles. Another quarter of an inch makes a lot of difference, so a five-and-a-quarter-inch bit would fit the largest muzzled horse

you care to ride. The rings should be quite close to the horse's lips without pinching them in. You can determine the size to get if you check the bit you now have to make sure it fits this way, then measure its mouthpiece. A bit that is too short naturally pinches the horse's lips, but one that is too long folds up so much in use that it hurts the horse.

A horse should not be put into the curb bit until he is thoroughly trained. Even then I would not use the curb unless I were showing in a class that gave me no alternative. Even when showing a trained horse in the curb, it is best to do most of your homework in the snaffle to keep him sweet and working right. Give him just enough curb bit work at home to keep him accustomed to it. So you see, that snaffle bit is very important.

The piece of equipment that goes with the snaffle is the dropped noseband, which is never used with the curb. It took me quite a while to accept this piece of tack because I was told it was to make the horse keep his mouth shut—I would have gladly used it on a person or two now and then! I was also told it made the snaffle more severe by forcing the horse to accept it on the bars of his mouth. Finally, I studied the setup and discovered that a properly adjusted dropped noseband takes some of the pressure off the mouth and puts it on the nose. It also stabilizes the snaffle—much to the horse's relief. I highly recommend this piece of equipment.

The selection of reins is important because you

Reins should be the right width to fit your hands comfortably with some friction between the knuckle and the first joint of the forefinger.

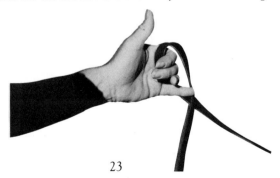

23

An excellent sport saddle showing the deep seat with the stirrups hung within five inches
of it. Stirrups here are tied up for longeing.

want to be able to hold them firmly in your hands
without creating any tension. While you seldom
want the reins to slip through your fingers, there are
times when this is necessary; so reins used in all
basic training should be smooth, not braided or
laced. Your own hands determine the width the
reins should be. Place the rein between the knuckle
and the first joint of your forefinger. When you
close your fist, you should feel a comfortable amount
of pressure contact with each edge of the rein. This
pressure is the main thing that keeps the rein from
slipping. If the rein is too narrow, you will have to
clamp your fist shut, causing tension. If it is too
wide, it will be uncomfortable when you close your
hand. Closed reins are less trouble than open ones

and ten feet total length is the proper length to fit
the average-size horse and let you give him the correct amount of freedom when needed.

Saddles! While the saddle does not make the
horse, an improperly proportioned saddle can prevent a person from ever becoming a secure, compe-
tent rider. I always cry inside when a person shows
up at class with a beautiful new saddle and I have to
tell him there is no way he will be able to sit properly in that saddle. Maybe right here I should give
you my definition of "proper." *It is the easiest way to
get the best results.* Oh, I know both the written and
unwritten rules on seats and saddles, but I also know
that you can win in stiff competition riding a "dressage seat" in either a dressage or stock saddle (ac-

An excellent stock saddle with the proper seat and stirrup leather placement. These fenders were shortened to allow the rider freer leg movement.

cording to class). This is a proven fact, so do not back off thinking you will give up those pretty blue ribbons if you follow my directions.

It does not matter whether you ride a stock saddle or an English saddle (hereafter arbitrarily referred to as a sport saddle). Either kind should have a good depression to put your seat in and the stirrups hung no farther forward of this depression than four or five inches. When the saddle is on the horse, it should be just high enough at the pommel and cantle to put you in the seat depression. The sport saddle should be well padded under the cantle to maintain this position. Saddles built up so high in front that they push you out the back door will not let you get your legs under you where they are the

most effective and give you the most secure seat.

The other thing is to get a saddle that fits you. The style in stock saddles nowadays is fifteen inches for a person only 5'4". This may be okay for what the dressage people call a chair seat, but is too big when you sit properly. I'm 5'6" and weigh 125 and I ride a 14-inch stock saddle and a 16-inch sport saddle. Both have a deep seat and stirrups hung close to it.

You'll need two whips—one for riding and one for longeing. The riding whip should be forty to forty-five inches long, not counting the short lash. If shorter than this, you cannot reach the horse's body behind your leg. The longeing whip should be six or seven feet long with a 9-foot or 10-foot lash. If you have such a whip with a short lash, you can lengthen it by tying leather boot laces together and onto the lash. The fiberglass whips are best because they hold their shape and are lighter to carry. If you are buying a longeing whip, hold it and flick it back and forth some to see if the weight and balance suit you. Too light a whip is difficult to control and too heavy a one tires you excessively.

The only other equipment needed is a longe line and side reins. If you want to go to the expense of buying a regular longeing cavesson, it works very well; but you can longe a horse very nicely by threading the line through the bit ring and over the horse's head. This longe line should be twenty-five feet long within a foot either way. Those on the market are very good if you get the stiff ones, not the soft, raggy ones.

Side reins should be six feet long unbuckled. From the bit snap to the buckle is usually about twenty-eight inches, and the end unbuckles all the way to let you put it around the girth or latigo. The holes should be evenly spaced and numbered. This saves a lot of counting.

One or two snaffle bridles, dropped noseband, reasonable saddle, two whips, longe line and side reins—isn't it nice to know that this is all the equipment you'll need until the horse is thoroughly trained? No gadgets or gimmicks to buy. No shopping around for a bit to suit the horse. Just good, sound training with this correct equipment makes you and your horse a happy team.

Part Two
Longeing

2

HANDLING THE LONGEING EQUIPMENT

Longeing is where the training starts. Not only is longeing an excellent training tool, but it is useful throughout the life of the horse. Its use for exercising the horse is obvious, but longeing can be considered a necessity in the schooling and conditioning of combined training horses, endurance horses, games horses and all types of show horses.

Longeing is of no value unless it is done correctly. You cannot do it correctly if you do not know the mechanics of it. I have run into difficulty teaching people to longe simply because they would not practice handling the equipment before they tried to apply it to the horse. You will do yourself and your horse a big favor if you will practice handling the equipment without the horse until you are proficient at it.

Handling the longe line requires practice, both for safety and for refined control of the horse. I do not care whether you fold the line or coil it. In either case you slip the loop at the end over your

This is the safest and easiest way to get the longe line under your fingers for better feel and control of the horse.

hand back to the palm. To fold you simply lay one fold across your hand one way and the next fold back the other way—back and forth until you have taken up the line. To feed out the line you let the top fold slip through your fingers. Eventually there comes the point where you would drop a fold if you let it slip farther. Use your whip hand to hold the line while you drop the fold so you can maintain reliable contact with the horse's head. To take up the line you must again use your whip hand.

To coil the line you make loops over and over again in the same direction across your palm and out over the back of your hand, making sure the one on top is always the one nearest the horse. In feeding these coils out you again let the line slip through your fingers, using your whip hand to hold the line while you drop the last of each coil. Do this before the coil gets anywhere close to being snug.

When I have my horse out on the circle where I want him, I always drop an extra coil. This gives me

all the adjusting room I need without the line hanging down where I might step in it. I also like to reverse the line in my hand at this time so it goes out toward the horse under my little finger. Without changing your hold on the coils, simply let the line come over the top of your pointer finger and close your other three fingers over the top of the line. I think this reversal gives me better feel of contact, but there are some who disagree with me on that. I use my whip hand to make these adjustments and to take up the coils just as in folding.

Folding is preferable to coiling when it comes to reversing the horse. You can simply put the folds into the other hand as long as they are not tangled. The coils must be reversed. I usually do this as I take up the line while walking up to the horse. I put the line in the other hand and coil it, making it in proper order for the new direction. (We do not reverse on the longe while the horse is in motion. For one thing, we have to reverse the line on his head if not using a longeing cavesson. For another, we want him to stop and stand on the circle—never come to us.)

If you are learning from scratch, you will probably want to fold the line. If you are experienced at coiling ropes, you may want to coil the line. Either way, attach your line to a fence or whatever, and practice handling the line until you can do it without looking directly at it. Back away as you feed out line and step forward as you take it up so you maintain a contact or light tension on it at all times. It is important to learn to handle the line reflexively and to maintain contact at all times.

You must also learn to handle the longeing whip. When the horse is going forward satisfactorily, you normally hold the whip behind him pointed slightly away from him and about two feet above the ground. Then you are in position to start the driving motion as needed. The proper driving motion is up and back, then down, forward and up—all smoothly done with wrist motion. At times when you must hit the horse, hit him on his heels as you start the final upswing. As you get more accurate, it is more effective in some instances to hit him on his body just behind the stirrup; but it is still on the final upswing. This complete motion lets you use the whip more smoothly, drives the horse's hind legs under him better, and educates him so that eventually just raising the whip up and back is usually sufficient to remind him to go forward.

Another motion you need to learn is bringing the whip forward smoothly on about the same level so that it is pointing at the horse's body or head. This is used when a horse tends to come in closer to you. The other things you do with the whip are to lower it pointed back of you, and to tuck it under your whip arm with the lash to the rear. Practice all of these motions with the whip until you can do them easily with either hand.

Now practice with both the line and whip. Stand at right angles to your "horse" with your whip hand closest to it and the line coming across your chest.

Line yourself up with the "horse's" flank or hip. This is how you will stand in relation to your horse when longeing. Always bend your longe-line elbow, carrying your fist up toward your shoulder. This gives you the greatest flexibility to shorten or lengthen the line with your arm. Practice feeding out and taking up the line along with the various whip motions, and practice using your whip hand to help in handling the line while maintaining the whip's position.

It would be a good idea to hang ribbons where the horse's heels and body would be to give you targets. Put a set of targets on each side of the "horse's" body so you can practice going both directions *as we always longe a horse equally in both directions.* In longeing you look at the horse's girth area most of the time so you can see the whole horse. Get so you can hit your targets without looking directly at them.

While you can use a surcingle to rig the horse for longeing, I prefer to saddle the horse so he gets used to working with the saddle on. I do not hobble the stirrups of a stock saddle. They will flop some but that just helps a horse get used to such things and become more calm. On the sport saddle the stirrups should be run up the leathers and the leathers then wrapped around and through the stirrups so they do not slip down. These stirrups would swing and flop enough to hurt the horse if left hanging. The side reins go around the latigos of the stock saddle or the girth of the sport saddle.

The horse is longed in the snaffle bit. The longeing cavesson shown is equipped with bit straps. If yours has no bit straps, put the bridle on first, then the cavesson, then slip the nosepiece of the cavesson under the cheeks of the bridle before buckling it around the horse's muzzle. The longe line is usually snapped into the center ring, although it can be snapped into the inside side ring on a horse that tends to lug.

You can longe quite effectively with just the bridle and dropped noseband. Run the longe line through the bit ring nearest you from the outside in,

Brian Bevan. Standing at right angle to his "horse," Brian maintains contact with the line and holds the whip in the passive driving position.

Brian maintains whip position while grasping the line so he can drop the shortened coil without dropping contact.

up over the horse's poll and snap into the bit ring on the other side. When you are going to reverse the horse, you must reverse this too. If the horse is especially touchy about the line attached to the bit, you can snap into the side ring of the dropped noseband or get a rubber bar snaffle to use until he has accepted the bit.

If you have reins on your bridle, get them safely out of the way by leaving them on the horse's neck and crossing them over each other two or three times under his throat. Then thread the throatlatch through one of them in the middle of this twist and buckle it up. (If the reins are open, first tie a knot in them about five feet from the bit.) The throatlatch should always be buckled quite loosely. If tight, it hampers the horse in bending at the poll. Chokes him where he flexes in other words!

Besides practicing with the equipment, you can be building a longeing pen. A horse can be longed in the open, but a pen of some sort makes the initial

training easier because it gives him—and you—a guide to follow. The longeing circle should have a diameter of at least fifty feet and no more than fifty-five feet. The area should be as level as possible. Use a stake and a 25-foot to 28-foot string or rope as a compass to mark out the circle.

Your fence can be as simple as logs six to eight inches in diameter and about six feet long laid around the circumference, or as complicated as a 2-by-4 wire mesh. Hog wire is unsuitable. An inexpensive, easy-to-make fence is made by driving metal posts about eight feet apart all around the circle and hanging pieces of old hose or plastic pipe on them at about the height of the horse's elbow. Or you can braid ropes out of all that baling twine or anything thick enough for the horse to see easily. Make one space a gate by attaching a ring or loop that can be slipped over the top of the post. If you use a fence corner or a square corral for longeing, block off each corner on the curve of your circle

The longeing cavesson properly adjusted. The noseband should be snug to prevent chafing but still just loose enough for the horse to chew pieces of carrot.

Tyke properly rigged for longeing with the reins tied up with the throatlatch, the longe line run through the bit and over his poll to snap in the off bit ring, the side reins adjusted for early training. The dropped noseband should be about half an inch higher on his nose.

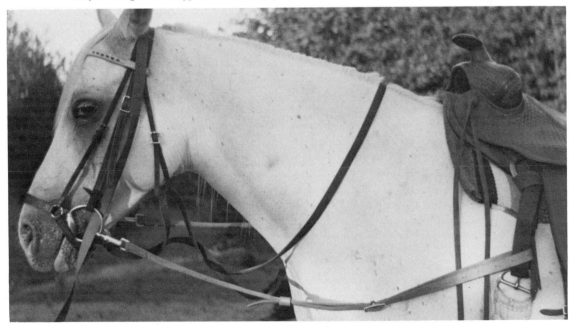

Cindy Flath and colt. Even though this colt did a lot of initial rushing, he respected this simple longeing pen. Cindy has good contact for control and is in proper position to go forward with the colt.

since the horse will tend to follow the fence wherever it goes.

Longeing greatly improves the performance of any saddle horse. We have a tendency to think we should be riding the horse to get on with his training. I know I used to feel this way; but I found out differently when I was forced to longe Dos for a month. He got a lump of some sort just behind his off elbow big enough and stubborn enough that I could not ride him but could longe him. All that month I felt I would be glad when I could get back in the saddle and go on with his training. I did longe him properly and thoroughly; and when I finally could get back on him, this horse with a naturally high head and low back, serious problems, went twice as good as when I left off riding!

Starting a colt with longeing puts you way ahead. For one thing, no colt is ready to be ridden before he is three years old. Those that are grown out early are

actually weaker than those that have been allowed to grow at a more normal rate. None of them are strong if they grow up in paddocks or flat pastures. Nothing develops a horse better than steep hills, rocks and brush to run in with just enough good feed, vitamins and minerals to keep him growing but not fat. So longeing gives you a chance to work him for six months to a year before he is old enough to start riding. I would not longe any horse before he is two.

For those of you who are starting colts, perhaps I should briefly mention the principles involved in getting them saddled and bridled. It is important to have any horse under control when working with him. Be sure your colt stands tied well; then during first saddlings, tie him with a strong rope to a strong post in a safe place. It is not that you want to force the saddle on him—just that you want to prepare for any emergency. Do not use a snap in your tie rope. Snaps break easily.

Every time you have handled the colt up to now, you should have gradually gotten him used to rub rags flopping around him, ropes dangling here and there and all such things that could frighten him. From that small start you can go on to flopping a gunny sack on and around him, *always going at the speed he can accept these things, never goosing him into exploding.* Then you can get him used to having the saddle blankets flopped on his back from either side. Then comes the saddle.

Do not try to sneak the saddle on him. Make sure he sees what you are doing. Horses do not like to be startled. They will accept all kinds of objects and noises if they have a chance to see them or the source. If you try to sneak things over on a horse, he will not develop confidence in you; and without that he will never become your partner.

Let him see the saddle and give him a chance to smell it and rub his lips on it. (Lips are his feelers.) Then rub it against his shoulder and lift it gently on his back. If you can use a lightweight saddle to start with, it will be a big help to you. Keep up a matter-

34

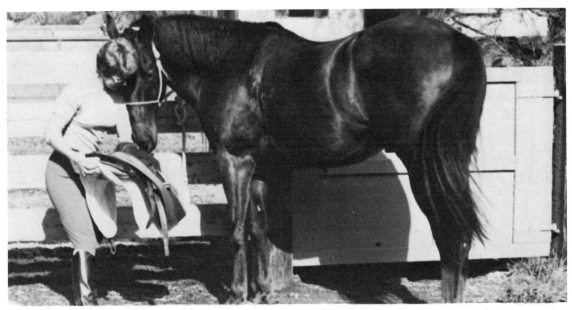

Peggy Barcaglia and Rafe. Let the colt see and feel the saddle. Never try to sneak anything over on a horse.

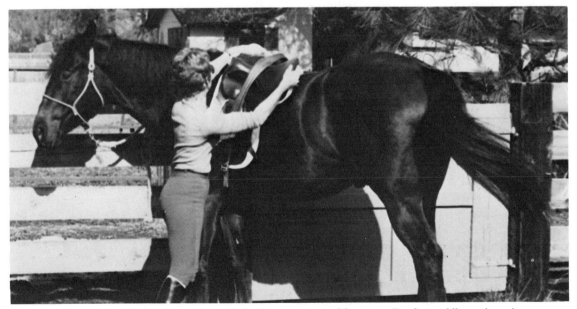

Place the saddle gently on the colt's back in a matter-of-fact way. For first saddlings the colt should have the rope tied into his halter instead of snapped.

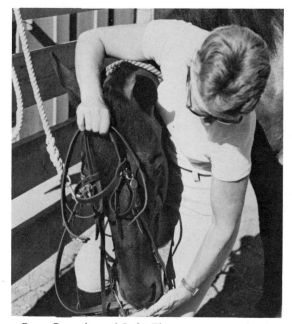

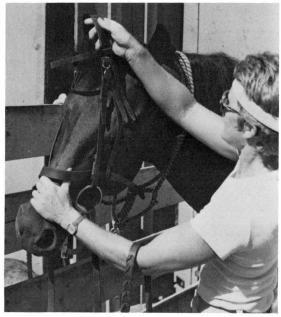

Peggy Barcaglia and Rafe. The proper way to bridle any horse. The hand holding the crown lifts the bit into the horse's mouth.

Always take care in unbridling to keep the horse's face in the vertical to avoid bumping his teeth.

of-fact conversation with him as you work. Talk him into standing while you check the off side and arrange the cinch. Take up the cinch slowly and smoothly until it is just snug enough to hold the saddle in place. No more. If he shows signs of discomfort during cinching, do not feel you must quickly get it tightened. Instead, stop and talk without letting go your hold on the saddle and cinch. Each time he relaxes some, you can continue.

Let him soak this up while you talk to him and straighten out things—whether they need it or not. Then let him know how it is going to feel to be cinched tighter by running your hand under the latigo or girth and tugging gently. Then take it up a little more. I remove the back cinch and introduce it this same way after a colt longes obediently. Sad-

dle him this same way for a week or more, and even then avoid cinching up with a jerk. Handle your horse with sympathy as well as firmness, and later on you will be able to cinch him up without his swelling up like a toad. That is caused by nervousness, not orneriness. So help him relax during saddling.

It is important that he relax for bridling too. Gradually get him so you can lay your right arm across the top of his head. Then for actual bridling, you can hold the crown of the bridle in your right hand and hold it in place this way. Smear some molasses on the bit, get in position, and let him smell it. Chances are very good he will decide to eat the goodies he smells. As he opens his mouth to eat the bit, slip it carefully into position by raising your right hand. Then finish bridling him, being careful

36

Iam reaches down to the bit and yields to it but can stand with his head at rest without leaning on the bit. A horse should not be bitted shorter than this without longeing him.

not to pinch his ears. If you must open his mouth, use your thumb against the roof of his mouth. He will open wide better that way.

I bridle a colt this way for quite some time, but there comes a time when he will probably take the bit quite willingly without the sweetener. You must also make sure to keep his face in the vertical as you remove the bridle. I hold the headstall with my right hand and keep his face vertical with my left hand on his nose. Then when he decides to spit the bit out, I lower the headstall. Bumping his teeth during bridling or unbridling can make a colt quite set against taking the bit.

You can leave a colt saddled and bridled for about an hour daily if you turn him loose in a corral where he cannot catch the reins on anything. Tie the reins to the saddle just barely snug when his head is at rest. Do not bit him any closer than this. We want the horse to learn to move into the bit on the longe, not stand around with his nose tucked in.

I would say that it will take you from two weeks to a month of regular daily practice to become well coordinated with the longe line and whip. Don't feel that this practice is a waste of time. I have seen horses very quickly learn to stop and face their trainers simply because they were well rewarded with standing while their handlers re-coiled the line to start over. Successful training requires concentration on the horse and reflex action—things you cannot do while trying to figure out how to use the equipment.

3

STARTING THE HORSE LONGEING

Before starting this novel experience of going around in circles and getting somewhere, you should know all the basic aids. It is not necessary to use verbal commands in longeing, and we certainly do not use them to eventually replace the whip and line aids. That would limit longeing to a mere exercise in obedience. Verbalizing can be a help to the trainer because of the subconscious relationship of his words to his actions. It can get unwanted results too. I was quite some time figuring out why my longe-trained colt would trot under saddle every time I said aloud, "I don't want you to trot here!"

Tone of voice is more important than which words you use, but be consistent in using the same words for the same action. In asking a horse to change to faster gaits or to move better, your voice should command obedience without shouting and the accent should be on the final syllable of the command. The reverse is true for shifting down or calming the horse. Your voice should be soothing and should trail off at the end of the command. In all cases speak with authority and confidence—no matter how frustrating things get!

During our longe lessons in our dressage clinics, Mr. Friedlaender would get exasperated trying to get us to make the horse stop dawdling around on the end of the line. To improve the horse and our understanding, he would longe the horse himself, getting him working and relaxed. Our turn again and the horse would almost immediately go back to dawdling, at which Mr. Friedlaender would boom from the sidelines, "MOVE that horse!" The horse, like a GI caught goldbricking, would immediately start going forward while we still stood there blank-faced. It takes practice and experience to become such a voice of authority. Do not get discouraged. It will come.

After the horse thoroughly understands going around you on the large circle, you can simply put him on the track, back off into position, raise the whip behind him and cluck to get him to walk on. (*Track is the trail on the outer limits of the longe circle or the arena. I will use it a lot so remember it.*) To ask for the trot from the walk use the command "Ta–rot." Say "Ta–" as you bring the whip back and up. Say "–rot" as you bring it forward, down and up. If he does not trot, repeat, and this time hit his heels with the lash. If he is more advanced in longeing, hit his body behind the stirrup.

To ask for the canter, be sure he is moving forward correctly in the trot. Bring his head slightly toward the inside without bringing him off the track. With his head slightly to the inside, raise the whip as you say "Can–." As you bring the whip down and forward, relax your longe line hand to let his head start back and say "–ter." Do not lose the contact as you relax your hand; but as he takes the canter, do let the line slip a little to compensate for the change of motion and speed. Your hand will have to follow his head motion to maintain contact without pulling him down to the trot.

To ask for the trot from the canter, keep the whip in the normal position and fix your hand—close your fist and stop hand motion—as you say "Ta-rot." If he does not trot immediately, relax your fixed hand and ask again, repeating until he responds. The moment he starts into the trot, prepare to drive him tactfully forward into an energetic trot.

To ask for the walk from the trot, turn the whip back away from him as you fix your hand and say "Wa-a-alk." Again be ready to drive him on in an energetic walk as he takes it. The halt is the same, except the coaxing command is "Ho–ho" and you tuck the whip under your whip arm, lash to the rear of you.

Never get stuck in the fixed hand—relax and ask again. Always be prepared to relax it the moment the horse appears to start the change. If he does not go ahead and change, you can ask again. Remember, too, that how you move affects how the horse moves. In teaching the horse to take the canter, it is helpful to squat a little as you raise the whip and bring it down. Then rise smoothly to the upright as you bring the whip up. It can also be helpful to canter or skip yourself, starting at the moment the horse should change to the canter. These things can be discontinued when he understands. If you march to a lively drummer, you can help activate his trot; but if you continue to move lively when asking him down to the walk, he will usually keep right on trotting. Stop yourself when asking him to halt.

To prepare the horse to longe, rig him complete with side reins. Snap the side reins together on top of his neck and tie a snap to the pommel of the saddle so they will not slip. For the first week or ten days of training, do not snap the side reins into the bit at the beginning of a lesson because the horse often makes sudden starts that would cause him to bump his mouth. After he settles into trotting around, he is ready for them, so we always go prepared. Even when he is fully trained, never lead him with the side reins snapped to the bit except during the process of longeing.

Put the longe line on the horse for going to the

Author and Iam. In training a horse to go on the longe you must drive him ahead with the whip—never lead him forward. Iam already understands longeing, so the side reins are attached and are the right length for a beginning horse.

left (counterclockwise) and lead him onto the track of the longe circle facing in that direction. Hold the coils, or folds, of the line in your left hand with the whip on top of them, butt forward, lash trailing out behind you. Stand beside the horse and behind his shoulder, facing in the same direction he is facing. Hold enough uncoiled line in your right hand to leave slack between your hand and his head.

At this time it is easier if the horse is not too complacent about the whip because *you want him to move forward away from it—you do not want to lead him forward.* Move the lash behind him, wiggle it, wrap it around his hind legs, tap him with the whip—progressing from a light aid to a stronger one until you get him to move. (Do not get it under his tail—he would move improperly!) When he starts forward, go with him, being careful not to tighten the line since you do not want to stop him.

Watch carefully to keep him moving by wiggling

the whip the amount necessary at the moment he starts to think about stopping. As he walks forward, let the line slip through your right hand so he gets ahead of you. When he is far enough ahead that you are even with his hips and moving in a steady walk, drop the line with your right hand and reach behind you to take the whip in it. As you do this, move away from the horse toward the center of the longe circle so your position is about even with his flank. Stay turned so you are facing in the same direction he is, otherwise you will be "chasing" him instead of walking with him. Be prepared to keep him moving forward by driving with the whip when necessary.

Gradually you can drop away more toward the center as you feed out more line, but not so far at this time that you cannot reach his heels with the whip. In keeping him moving forward, use the whip by degrees. Start by bringing it back and up. If he goes forward better, fine. All you have to do is lower

41

Cindy Flath and colt. When the colt understands
walking ahead of you and the whip, reach behind to
take the whip in your driving hand as you keep going.
Be sure to face forward, otherwise you will end
up chasing the horse.

cept it and seek it. So initially it is a come-and-go
thing with your doing all the work. Eventually, if
your work is thorough and correct, the horse will
move out on a larger circle as you let out the line.
Without contact you have no control. With it you
can develop almost psychic control.

Taking the contact is very touchy at first because
you do not want to jerk him and discourage the very
thing you are teaching him—going forward. Keep
in mind that you are longeing—not playing hot
walker. *Always be willing to move your hand forward
and/or let the line slip a little (yielding). Always be
prepared to bend the elbow—to take up the lost contact.
These must be done smoothly.* If the horse charges
ahead while you have contact and you don't yield
your hand and/or the line so you slow him gradually,
he will hit it and turn toward you. If you're longeing
in the open and you've lost contact, he can whirl
away from you. With lost contact he is also more
likely to charge and then hit the end and whirl
toward you. Even if he doesn't flip around, he'll get
discouraged about going forward and that makes
more work for you.

After you have taken the whip in your right
hand, anytime the horse goes into the trot encourage him to keep trotting. If he doesn't offer, coax
him into the trot as soon as possible. If you aren't
walking forward with the horse, you'll find yourself
"chasing" him, which can cause him to get excited
and "run away." If you have got unyielding contact,
you won't be able to keep up and you will pull him
around facing you. If you don't have contact, he will
hit the line and turn. *So be sure to be walking forward
with him, not toward him.* (Are you beginning to see
why you need so much practice with the equipment!)

When you take the contact, the horse usually
makes the circle smaller. Continue to take the contact lightly and bring the whip smoothly forward so
you point it at his middle or his head. Wiggle the
whip if necessary. As he moves out from the whip,
walk out with him to enlarge the circle. Each time

it to the normal position behind him. If he does not
respond, bring it down, forward and up near his
heels. If that does not get response, do it again and
lash his heels lightly. *Always apply aids this way,
lightly, then gradually stronger until you get the desired
results.* Hitting the horse with the whip is certainly
permissible if he is lethargic—or later on, disobe-
dient. He has to know that the whip means business. But study your horse to know if, when and
how strong he needs it. *Never use the whip in anger.*

During all this you also have to take contact on
the longe line—probably at the time you first move
away from the horse, though it can be sooner. Contact is a very difficult thing to explain without actual demonstration. *It is a firm but soft, elastic feel
between your hand and the horse's head. Your hand
should feel neither empty nor loaded.* At first you cannot get this feel because you have to maintain the
contact yourself in order to teach the horse to ac-

42

Author and Iam. Point the whip at the horse's body or head to get him to make the circle larger and to maintain contact. If necessary, wiggle the whip or hit the horse on his body.

he responds, take the whip back to its normal position. Right from the beginning, start teaching him contact by taking it, yourself and encourage him to stay on the track by constantly moving him out to it.

Some horses start out leaning on the line. Still maintain the contact even though it is heavy. Just be sure you do not fix your hand. Relax it and close it so he does not have your unyielding support. After he understands to go forward in the trot (which will probably be within a matter of minutes), you can start teaching him not to lean so hard by smoothly and firmly pulling his head six to eight inches toward you and dropping contact for a brief instant. These are the motions of jerking without the jerk. Repeat again and again as needed.

After you have established his trotting forward willingly and relaxed, ask him to walk. After walking him on for a few feet, ask him to halt on the track still facing forward. Merely fix your hand again

and again. If you try to pull him to a stop, he will turn and face you. If he is slow to halt, start taking up line as you walk toward his head; continue to walk up to him when he is halted so he will not be tempted to move on or turn. Maintain contact without pulling as you walk toward him. If he turns toward you anyway, turn him back onto the track before petting him.

Change your line to the opposite side if you are not using a cavesson; make sure your line is in order for going to the right (clockwise) and take up your position on his right with whip and coils in your right hand and loose line in your left. Start him forward the same way as you did on the near side. As he moves, guide him through a change through the circle. We do not turn the horse around in place because that would be difficult for him later on when he is working in shortened side reins. Use the whip behind him to keep him moving as you guide him through this change.

43

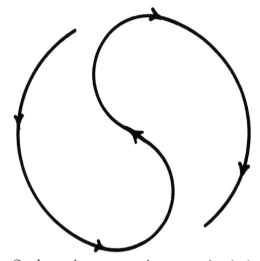

On the track you can get him going ahead of you and then drop away, taking the whip in your left hand and keeping him going forward. In going on this hand, follow all the instructions I have given you for going to the left. Get him trotting and keep him going until he is going forward willingly and relaxed. If the initial training was difficult for you and the horse, and all this has taken nearly an hour, loosen his cinch when you halt him and put him away.

If he caught on quickly —say in half an hour— change back to the left with a change through the circle and halt him so you can snap the side reins into the bit. *Side reins are always adjusted equal length.* At this time, they should be adjusted loose when his neck is level with his body and his head relaxed. Longe him each way in the trot for five or so minutes —until he is going forward well and relaxed. When the lesson is over, unsnap the side reins and loosen the cinch before leading him out of the longeing area.

In teaching my students to longe their horses, I found a certain pattern of difficulties. Number one was the lack of ability to handle the equipment. If you have to concentrate on how to feed out and take up line and how to move the whip, you cannot concentrate on what the horse is doing and encourage or correct him before it is too late. The second biggest problem was getting the student to understand that the whip drives the horse ahead of him and the longe line merely limits the scope of the horse's travels.

The third problem is related to the second. Without taking contact on the longe line you cannot control where the horse goes. The secret of training a horse to longe is to keep him moving forward with the whip while catching and directing that energy with the line. If the horse cuts in, you drive him with the whip from behind or in his middle as you pick up the contact with your arm, stepping back if necessary. If the horse swerves out, you drive with the whip as you take on the line again and again, but avoid pulling his head in.

The one time you do not need to drive is when the horse goes rushing around like crazy. He is already moving so keep the whip pointed away from him and maintain contact even if it means keeping him on a small circle for a while. Work to slow him down and then stop him and attach the side reins. Attach them so they are just taut when his head is at rest. They will help control the horse and control is essential whether it is making him slow down or speed up.

Right from the beginning start encouraging the horse to perform in the same way you will expect him to perform under saddle—going forward willingly under control, rhythmic, relaxed, straight and later, balanced. The horse that is quite lethargic will understand better that you can make him move if you do not delay in giving him one smart crack on the heels with the whip. This teaches him to respect it and makes less work for you. The horse that goes tearing frantically around you needs to be coaxed into slowing down. Hold the whip back away from him and take rhythmically on the longe line as you tell him "E-a-s-y," over and over to get him to settle down.

When you get either type of horse moving forward under your control, he will still be rushing, as evidenced by his short, quick strides, higher head carriage, and stiff tail carriage. Just start working for rhythm, urging the horse forward with the amount of whip action your particular horse needs just as he starts to slow, and encouraging him not to rush off at runaway speed by taking and yielding on the line as he starts to rush off.

When you can get him to maintain a steady rhythm, he will begin to relax. Watch for the lowering of his head, longer strides and a slowing of the rhythm without much loss of forward speed. If the horse is simply losing his energetic trot, his strides behind will be short and lazy instead of reaching far forward and pushing. You can check his tracks to see that his hind feet are stepping in the tracks of his front feet. This indicates that he is working. The horse's tail is a good indicator, too. When he relaxes but is still working, his tail starts relaxing and the tail hairs ripple in rhythm with his strides. By recognizing the difference between relaxation and mere loss of energy, you avoid punishing him for relaxing by driving him forward with the whip.

You can help a horse establish a slower rhythm while maintaining energetic strides by clucking to him in the rhythm you want for several strides each time you feel him start to lose energy. Another help is to roll the lash of the whip toward his middle like a hoop, doing this about every fourth stride. An overhand flip of the wrist will make that lash go into a loop that rolls out to the end. Try it without the horse until you master it.

The moment the horse starts trotting on the longe you start working for energy and rhythm as well as keeping him on the track and maintaining contact. As soon as you feel that he understands that you want him to go around you on the longe circle, you start working for energy in the walk; but never keep him in the walk for more than twice around at a time. Also start asking for obedience by not letting him trot on until you tell him or stop trotting except on command.

You also want the horse to travel straight. Straight on a circle? Sure! *A horse is straight when his hind feet go forward on the same lines as their respective front feet. So, on a curve his spine must be bent full length, otherwise his feet would travel on different lines. You do not get him to bend by shortening the inside side rein – these are always adjusted equal length.* This gives you one check to see that he is properly bent—and therefore straight—because the inside side rein will hang looser than the outside one. You also check to see that his hind feet are stepping on their respective front tracks. Both of these must check out so you know he is not overbending in the neck or dropping his hindquarters out to avoid bending in the middle of his body.

After his first two to four lessons, the horse should begin accepting contact, staying on the track well and going forward relaxed with rhythm. However, you will find he needs at least five minutes of trotting in each direction at the beginning of each lesson to get limbered up. Don't bug him during the limbering up other than to ask him to go forward well, maintain contact and develop rhythm. When he relaxes going to the left, switch to the other hand and finish the limbering up so he is traveling with long, rhythmic strides, tail swinging.

Then you can snap the side reins into the bit and start straightening the horse—that is, bending him. You ask him to bend with a slight take and yield on the line, maintaining contact as you keep him working correctly. At the same time, point the whip at his body behind the cinch to encourage him to bend his body. Do not let him go unbent. Instead, subtly correct him again and again as he starts to unbend. Do not expect him to stay bent on a small circle. Keep him on the track.

You also want him to lower his head. This develops his back muscles and hind quarters and helps him stride under. *Whenever he stretches his head down for any reason—even to cough or smell the ground— praise him for it. Do not think for a minute that you can pull his head down—or set it—with the side reins. This*

Peggy Barcaglia and Tyke. Tyke is relaxed, rhythmic, striding under and stretching down.
Now Peggy can gradually shorten the side reins—always equal length—to help Tyke
reach the bit. Working on getting more bend in his body will lighten the contact. The horse
must learn to stretch down like this in the initial training under saddle, too.

is not acceptable.

Bending and lowering the head are interrelated, so you ask the horse to stretch down the same way you ask him to bend. He must be energetic, rhythmic and relaxed and the side reins must be attached to bring the outside one into contact. With my high-headed horse I used to verbalize, saying, "lower your head" as I asked him with the line and whip to bend and stretch down. Then one day as I was warming him up under saddle and he was going in his usual initially tense, high-headed way, I said, "lower your head." His head went "plonk" right down on a level with his body! I was quite surprised—and pleased!

For the first week or ten days, while you are getting the horse to understand the basics of longeing,

warm him up without the side reins snapped to the bit. After that you can start his lessons with them attached. Snap them on when you are at the longeing pen ready to work and unsnap them before leading the horse away at the end of work.

Pay attention to all the details in the order I have given them. Praise the horse liberally. Control him rather than punish him. Always work equally both directions with frequent changes. If he volunteers the canter—not running away—do not discourage him in it. He will not canter on long. But do not feel that you are not making progress if you do not canter him right away, as some horses need a month or more of trot work first. From the energetic, rhythmic, relaxed trot comes the ability to canter easily.

4

TRAINING THROUGH LONGEING

The things we teach a horse on the longe are the things we want him to learn under saddle. A well-trained riding horse is what dressage people call "between your legs and your hands" or "on the aids." This means he respects your leg aids and yields to the bit so well that you can put him through all the gaits and maneuvers you have taught him with practically invisible use of your legs (and related aids) and your hands. Old-timers would say, "He's right up on the bit!"

On the longe we put the horse between the whip—a substitute for the rider's legs—and the hand through the longe line. However, the longe line by itself would not do the job because it would make the horse respond to an inside rein only and encourage him to bend his neck instead of his entire spine. We put side reins on the horse to give him guidelines to step between, to make it possible for him to reach the bit when he stretches down and seeks contact with it, and to train him to "go on the outside rein." The horse that will stretch into the outside rein will automatically turn a smooth corner when that rein is yielded a fraction of an inch as the horse is driven forward with the rider's inside leg. He is not turned with the inside rein and for this reason we always adjust the side reins equal length so he longes on the outside contact only.

Side reins also give us the means to train the horse to yield to the bit and flex at the poll instead of in the middle of his neck, as he does when his head is "set." When you take a little on the longe line, this tightens the outside rein. Since only one side of the bit is pulled straight back (the line pulls to the side), the horse cannot lean on the bit but must tuck his nose. Because the horse is moving forward rhythmically and relaxed and you are not using force, the horse relaxes his jaws to yield. Because you can control his movement and the amount of tightening on the reins and line, you can prevent his over-flexing and thus bending in the middle of his neck. This is prevented by relaxing the longe line slightly as you encourage him to move forward better.

You will use the same principles of these aids and training when you ride the horse. That's why correct longeing can be so valuable in training the horse—he can get a head start on proper work without having to learn to carry your weight at the same time.

When you longe the horse, you're beginning this training by putting him between the whip and the longe line so you can just squeeze your hand shut and relax it to ask for the various things I told you to get by taking on the line. During all longeing, keep him going forward with the amount of whip aid needed. Be consistent, asking him with the aids as you see him start to come off them but relaxing them the moment he starts to obey so he stays responsive to them.

When your horse consistently works well on the longe, you can let out enough line that you can stand in the center of the longe circle, using your inside leg (left leg with the horse going to the left and vice versa) as a pivot point. This helps you keep the circle round unless you let him wander out as he chooses. While you should be willing to let the line slip through your hand to avoid jerking him, remember that you are longeing him, not the other way around. Keep him on the track firmly without jerking. (If you did not make a longeing pen, markers on the ground will help you keep track of the track.)

When the horse is stretching down well—lowering his head and then bringing it back up to about level with his body—you can shorten the side reins so they are just taut when he is standing at rest. This allows him to reach the bit and begin to seek contact with it. The contact should be only on the outside side rein when he is properly bent. It should not be stretched tight indicating that he is leaning on it, but it should not swing like the inside one, either.

After this, if your horse is continually stretching his head down, raising it up level or above his body and stretching it down again, he probably would like to maintain contact with the bit but is unable to do so in such a long frame. Try shortening the side reins one to three holes. Experiment to see where he seems to work the most comfortably. For about a week warm him up on the former adjustment, shortening the side reins to the new setting when he is ready to begin work. After that just start him out on the new length.

Sometimes it is difficult to get a horse to stretch down. Often you can help this horse by shortening the side reins enough that his face is pulled in nearly to the vertical. Then longe him this way for several trotting circles, making sure he steps well under and is relaxed and rhythmic. When you see him tuck his nose several times, lengthen the side reins so they are just taut when he is at rest and see if he will then stretch all the way down. Do it going both ways. If he does not tuck his nose in two or three tries, just go back to working for the stretching in the original

Kathy Hansen and Watirah. Even though more advanced in longeing, any horse
will need initial warming up. Note high head and low back, short strides and
counterbending, tension evident in tail.

Now warmed up, Watirah is striding under and relaxed—note rippling tail—and has
lowered her head, which raises her back.

way. If this exercise with shortened side reins is overdone, it can affect the horse so he will not go up to the bit at all—called "behind the bit."

Both people and horses get bored with longeing. The horse may try to relieve the boredom by throwing in tricks after the first fifteen or twenty minutes. He may throw up his head and run off, or buck, or suddenly turn and face you—all sorts of tricks to liven things up. Usually the horse will have a favorite spot on the longe circle for this. Watch for signs such as rolling eyeballs, attention to the outside and slowing down. As he is approaching his chosen "playground," momentarily maintain firmer contact as you move him forward better without exciting him. That will remind him that you are the boss.

Work over a cavalletto can relieve the boredom and get the horse stretching better so he'll seek contact better. The cavalletto should be a solid log six to eight inches in diameter or a 4-inch pole or rail raised to the 6-inch or 8-inch height and solidly secured to its supports. It should be placed on a radius line of the longe circle so the horse can cross it from either side without changing his circle. Use it after the horse is warmed up and walk him across it a few times to let him get the feel of it. The side reins should be unsnapped until he has learned to trot across easily.

The first few times you trot him over the cavalletto, it's advisable to let him slow down if he wants so he can get used to it. After he shows he can handle it, always drive him whenever necessary to maintain his speed and rhythm as he approaches. Don't excite him—although by now he should respond to driving without excitement—as this would make him put his head up and his back down, thus defeating your purpose. Also, he should be staying on the track so you can prevent his cutting in around the pole.

This exercise makes the horse push more with his hind legs, arch his back, lower his head and carry himself better. When he has the feel of trotting over the pole, he can go on long side reins. When he carries himself well, the side reins can be shortened so he can reach the bit.

You can also use two or three cavalletti to further this training and to help a short-strided horse step farther under. These are placed on radii of the longe circle four feet apart at their centers (up to 4'6" for horses over 16.2 hands), and their centers should be placed on the track. Introduce the horse first to one, then two, then three so he can learn how to get across them. This spacing is for trotting only so do not ask him to walk or canter through them. This is not a trail class obstacle course. If your poles are long enough to accommodate a 2'4" spacing toward the center, you can walk him across there.

When your short-strided horse can handle three cavalletti slightly inside the track, move him out to the wider spacing and drive him as he approaches. This will make him stretch out to get across and so lengthen his stride. Gradually you can move him farther out. Always do this work after he is warmed up, and gradually build up the number of times you do it; otherwise you will make his muscles sore. Always work him both directions equally. It is hard work for him, so use judgment not to overdo it.

Cavalletti work also helps a horse develop balance and impulsion. Balance means that he shifts his weight toward the rear so that he carries himself more with his hindquarters. All horses must be balanced this way before they can be light on the bit and highly maneuverable. Impulsion is one step farther than going forward willingly. It is going forward with springy steps that push the horse lightly off the ground, making him a pleasure to ride. A horse must start to balance (carry himself) in order to start to develop impulsion. A horse running loose will do all these things at times. Our job is to show him we want him to do them when we ask and to develop them in an orderly fashion so he becomes physically able to do them under our added weight. On the longe he can learn and develop without that burden.

Watirah takes the trot cavalletti placed on radii of the longe circle. Note the improvement of the whole horse as she moves with more impulsion and better balance. Side reins can be attached after the horse learns to take the cavalletti in stride.

There are other exercises that help the horse develop balance and impulsion. Transitions are changes of gait or length of stride. Do not try this latter until all other things are well established. Then you can drive him onto the longe line, either softly restraining him for shortened strides or leading him with your hand to stretch out for lengthened strides. Be sure the rhythm stays the same as his regular rhythm; otherwise the exercise is incorrect.

As soon as he changes from walk to trot to walk easily, you can work him on walk-trot transitions, gradually decreasing to five walk and ten trot strides over and over. As soon as he takes the canter easily without excitement, you can work him on canter-trot transitions, gradually decreasing to ten trot strides and ten canter bounds over and over. Walk-to-canter, halt-to-trot, and halt-to-canter transitions are far more difficult for him both physically and mentally, so do not try them too soon.

You no doubt noticed that during this early training your horse would fling himself upward to go into the trot from the walk, or into the canter from the trot. In coming down to the trot from the canter, he probably took several rushing steps of trot and was inclined to coast down to a dying walk when asked to walk. These actions are caused by lack of strength and lack of balance.

As you longe him daily, his strength will improve. As he accepts contact on the longe line and gets in the habit of working instead of dawdling or rushing, his balance will improve some. Then you can help him in his transitions by squeezing your hand shut to strengthen the contact as you ask for changes upward. This will help him balance more so he can lift himself into the gait instead of having to

51

leap into it. Do the same in asking for transitions down, driving him lightly so he pushes into the change instead of simply falling into it and so having to rush forward or coast down to catch his balance. This will make it easier to get good transitions later on under saddle.

Another balancing exercise is the spiral which also asks him to bend more for several strides. When he accepts contact on the longe line so well that he will move out on a larger circle as you feed out line, you can bring him gradually in closer and then gradually move him out to the track again—all the while keeping him trotting well and maintaining rhythm. Be sure you get him to decrease the size of the circle by his obedience, not by pulling him in. At first make the circle just slightly smaller and build him up to making it much smaller. He has to stretch his muscles gradually.

There are two other problems that are likely to arise. One is getting the proper lead in the canter. If the horse is properly bent on the circle at the time he takes the canter, he will take the proper lead. This is one reason you help him by bending him just slightly more for taking the canter. The other reason is that this same request for bend will be used under saddle. If he takes the wrong lead, quietly ask for the trot and try again, being sure to bend him properly. If he goes disunited, you have probably asked at an awkward moment. The remedy is the same.

Disunited is the proper term for cantering on one lead behind and the other in front. Nowadays I hear it called crossfiring. Crossfiring is when a horse strikes his forefoot with his opposite hind foot. Only lateral gaited horses (pacers) can do this since they are the only ones that are bringing a left hind foot forward when the right forefoot is back and vice versa.

This brings us to the second problem, forging. Trotters forge, striking the forefoot with the hind foot on the same side. When your horse forges on the longe—and later on under saddle—do not ask your shoer to correct it. The horse is not yet balanced; and when he is, he will no longer forge. He may forge during warmup for quite some time, but he will stop it as soon as he can shift his weight toward the rear and so be able to move his front feet out of the way in time. He has to develop responsiveness to your aids in order to balance back when you ask. He has to develop his hindquarters and back muscles to be able to stay balanced for any length of time.

Have you started thinking this dressage stuff is all work and no fun? A lot of us think it sooner or later—usually when we hit a snag or do not seem to be making any progress. Then things break loose and start improving again. That is when we corner everybody we can to brag about our horses. Remember that any horse training is work for quite awhile and that the reward is a horse that easily does what you want most of the time. Remember that longeing is not preparing your horse for a career as a merry-go-round horse, but is developing and training him to make the work go that much faster under saddle. Correct longeing also develops mutual trust between you and your horse—an absolutely necessary ingredient for the very best performance.

So relieve the boredom with the various exercises, increase the enjoyment with frequent praise of your horse and hang onto your friends by controlling your bragging.

Part Three
Basic Training

5

SEAT, HOW TO AID, AND EXERCISES

Before you can hope to get the best results in training your horse, you need to learn how to sit on him to make it easiest to aid him. I am not going to talk about equitation seats other than to say that once you have mastered the so-called "dressage seat," you can revert to the equitation seat of your choice for the brief moments in equitation classes. There is no reason to change back in performance classes because there it is the horse that is being judged. In fact, sitting properly (the easiest way to get the best results) will improve your chances of scoring big.

There are three things basic to becoming a proficient rider-trainer. The rider must be relaxed, in balance with the horse, and have good feel of the horse. If you are not relaxed, you cannot apply the aids effectively. If you are not in balance with the horse, you will continually upset his balance, making it difficult for him to do his best work. If you do not have feel of the horse, your reactions will always be too late, either allowing the horse to have his own way or punishing him for doing the right thing. Feel should eventually be developed so you can maintain finer performance throughout the ride, rather than merely correct the gross errors.

To be relaxed on the horse, you must sit equally on both seatbones and feel your weight fully down on them. Relaxation, however, does not mean limpness. Muscles must be engaged but not tense. All the things you have heard about head and chest up, shoulders back, elbows hanging from your shoulders close to your body—all these things are correct. Two others are not. "Heels down" has been emphasized, I am sure, in an effort to keep people from hanging on with their legs and toes. Try sitting relaxed on your horse and then shove your heels down hard and see what it does to your seat. Pushes you right away from the saddle, doesn't it! All riding must be done with your seat as close to the saddle as possible. The only way to achieve this is in letting your weight keep you there through relaxation and letting the weight of your feet on the stirrups keep your heels and ankles relaxed.

The other thing you must watch: that in keeping your back straight, you really do. Too often a person "straightens" his back through coming to "a-tension." This puts an arch in the back and tilts the top of the pelvis forward. This in turn pushes the buttocks toward the rear and inhibits the forward motion of the horse. It also reduces relaxation and the ability to use the back. You must be supple in your back to ride well, so simply stretch upward to straighten up, making your pelvis straight up and down and letting your stomach hang loose so you are relaxed in the waist.

To be in balance with the horse, you obviously must sit equally on either side of his backbone. Feeling equal weight on your seatbones tells you that you're there. But you also must sit over his center of balance. If your pelvis is tipped forward pushing your seat out behind you, you would have to sit practically up on his withers to get your weight over

his center of balance—not a very feasible way to ride a saddle horse safely. So, if you now ride forward seat with your backside out back or chair seat with your knees out front, change these by bringing your seat into place over the area about eight to ten inches behind the horse's withers. Let your knees come down and back. This opens the angle between the front of your thighs and your pelvis.

Now, sitting relaxed with your knees slightly bent, you should find that your heel, your hip, your shoulder and your ear are all in a vertical line. In this position you are in balance with the horse and can hope to stay in balance regardless of what he does. When you master this position, you will find it is more secure than any other and can be maintained with shortened stirrups for jumping and lengthened stirrups for "English." Just keep your knees lowered and your heels in a line directly under your seatbones no matter how bent or open your knees are.

The other position used in some cross country riding and in initial training is what I call the "forward position"—not to be confused with the forward seat. To get in the forward position, push your knees and heels down as you bend your knees more and bend forward from your hip joints—not from your waist. Your position is proper when your crotch just clears the saddle and you can stay there at any gait without hanging on. If you fall forward or back, your heels are not directly under you. In this position it is easy to stay in balance with a green horse that is still on his forehand. You can post or simply let your knees and ankles take up the shock of the trot.

If you sit down from this position by simply straightening up so your weight rolls onto your seatbones and do this without changing the position of your legs, you will then be sitting properly in the straight down, relaxed position. Taking the forward position and then straightening up without changing leg position is a good way to get yourself in position each time you mount your horse.

The author and Iam. The "dressage" or balanced seat: knees lowered, inside leg "on the girth," heel, hip, shoulder and ear in a vertical line. There is tension in my legs as evidenced by the toe turned out and the pant leg crept up. Hands could be lowered some.

The chair seat: knees out in front pushing the rider behind the horse's center of balance. I am using an inside leading rein on this corner.

The forward position useful in riding out on trails and keeping weight off a colt's back. Note that my elbows are bent a little even with my hands on the horse's neck. This permits relaxation and a soft contact.

Sitting on the horse relaxed with your knees lowered, you should point your toes straight ahead or nearly so—not for the sake of having them point forward but because the insides of your upper calves should contact the horse. When your toes turn out, your whole leg is turned out and is ineffective; and it is a pretty good sign that your legs are not relaxed—that you are probably hanging on with them. Take the forward position, making sure your toes are pointed ahead and then sit down and let your legs stay relaxed. Stretch your legs down without pushing on the stirrups. These two things will roll your whole leg into position. Do this several times each ride until your legs stay in place. Do not ever try to force yourself into position since that destroys relaxation.

You should post the trot regardless of the type of saddle until the horse starts swinging his back and invites you to sit. To post easily you let the horse push you up; as that happens, you simply swing your pelvis forward through your elbows, leading with your stomach and raising your chest. To sit on the next stride, just relax into normal position so that you let yourself sit straight down. Do not lean forward, push down on the stirrups or grip with your knees. *Posting properly makes it easy, keeps you over the horse's center of balance and keeps the horse moving forward.*

Feel of the horse means that *without looking* you can tell what foot is going forward, what lead he is on, what his head and mouth are doing, whether he is tense or relaxed, straight and balanced, etc. But most of all, you can tell what he is thinking about doing next. When you are relaxed and in balance, you can develop feel more and more by glancing to see what the horse is doing and then paying close attention to how it feels.

Observing him from the ground also helps to show you what his body does when he moves. For instance, when his right hind leg goes forward, his body swings to the left. When you are on the horse, you can easily feel his body movement and so tell which hind leg is going forward. With good feel of the horse, you can apply the aids according to what is necessary at the moment and so get the smoothest performance from him.

Aids are the language we use to communicate with our horse and to let him communicate with us. They are not pushbutton cues. Rather they are logical and simple "words" that can be put together to form a large variety of "requests" to the horse. I will give you the mechanics (words) now and define the specific combinations (requests) later as needed.

Rein aids are just as important as the rest of the aids but detrimental if over-used or used alone. It is important to put them in their proper place since almost all of us mistakenly figure that as the head goes, so goes the horse. This just is not so. A great many of us have had the experience of turning a horse's head around almost to our knee and still have him run off in the opposite direction. *The most important thing about rein aids is to use them the least amount possible, indicating and yielding rather than demanding.*

The reins must be held coming from the horse's mouth into your fists between the little and ring fingers, up across your fingers close to your palms and out across the tops of your pointers between the knuckle and the first joint. Thumbs close down on top of the reins to hold them in position. Hold your hands thumbs up or nearly so, and keep your wrists and arms relaxed. Reversing the reins so they come in on top of your hands makes it necessary to move your whole hand to aid the horse and so startle and over-steer him. Hold the reins firmly—but not tensely—in your hands. Limp hands that hold the reins like a cup of tea at a social are not light hands. *Light hands yield (soften by relaxing the fingers slightly) when the horse yields.*

During work, contact must be maintained. Contact, remember, is a firm but soft, elastic feel between your hands and the horse's mouth. Holding the reins properly and maintaining contact, you can aid the horse simply by squeezing your hands shut or

The direct rein in my left hand comes straight back from the horse's mouth, while my right hand is turned with my thumb pointing at the horse's left ear. This brings the rein closer to his neck—the indirect rein.

Vicki Navarra and Mission Ridge. The leading rein: this turns the horse without restricting his hind leg on the same side.

by relaxing them, and at times rolling your hand. This is all that is needed to let the horse know what is wanted up front when he reliably seeks contact with the bit.

There are three kinds of rein aids:

(1) The *direct rein.* This is a simple tightening straight from the horse's mouth. Simply squeeze your fist shut on the rein. The outside rein is usually a direct rein. (Inside—the side toward which the horse is bent. Outside—the opposite side.)

(2) The *indirect rein.* This comes slightly against the horse's neck so the tightening of the rein is not straight back. It is usually used inside. You get the indirect rein by rolling your fist so you can see your fingernails and so your thumb is pointing toward the horse's opposite ear, or by keeping your thumb up and moving your whole hand slightly toward your opposite shoulder. Both movements are slight, just enough to flex the horse's head without bending his

neck. The indirect rein indicates direction without restricting the stride of the corresponding hind leg.

(3) The *leading rein.* Just rotate your forearm out from the elbow, turning your fingernails up and thumb out. Maintain contact as you do this. It gives the effect of your being on the ground and turning the horse from the side. It is used to the inside to help a green colt turn without bending his neck or restricting his stride. To use the leading rein start your hand out to the side. The moment you start getting the turn, start bringing your hand back. Move it back and forth the amount needed to get the turn. Never just stick it out there steadily until the turn is completed.

Practice these three "reins" and get them well fixed in your mind. They are indispensable training tools.

Body control, not strength, is needed to use any of the aids. Sit on your saddle horse and try an experiment.

Position yourself as I described, staying relaxed with your calves resting on the horse's sides. Now, without taking your knees away from the horse, move your feet straight out away from his sides a few inches. Then, without actually kicking him, kick them against his sides toward the rear the way most people kick a horse. Notice that this forces your pelvis to tip forward raising your seat off the saddle. Do the same thing again except kick straight onto the horse into the original leg position. Notice that this not only keeps your seat down, but tends to pull it deeper into the saddle.

That is the way you close your legs on the horse to move him forward—straight in without turning your toes out or moving your feet toward the rear of the horse. If your horse moves forward during any of this experiment, pet him; do not discourage him.

There are only two positions for your legs: (1) The normal position, called "on the girth" which is actually just barely behind the girth or cinch; and (2) Your foot moved about four inches farther back. I am going to arbitrarily call these: (1) the *driving position* or *driving leg,* because it is used to drive the horse forward; and (2) the *outside leg* or *outside position* because it is usually used outside. So from now on you will know what I mean by these two terms. *Never use your legs forward of the cinch.*

The outside leg is used to prevent the haunches from moving out on circles and turns. It is also used to cause the haunches to move over in such things as turn on the forehand, sidepass and halfpass. To put your leg in this position simply bend your knee, letting your lower leg slide back on the horse's side without pulling your heel up. When your horse understands this aid, it is all that is needed to hold the haunches in place. To aid actively for moving the haunches over simply roll your heel up the horse's side in a massaging motion or tap with your heel using the ball of your foot as a pivot point. Roll or tap your heel as his body swings away (that hind leg stepping forward) and relax it as his body swings back.

Your back is an important part of your riding anatomy because it ties all your aids together, giving you harmonious control of the horse. With your back muscles relaxed your seat can go with the motion of the horse's back while your upper body remains independent. Tightening your back muscles from your shoulders down through the small of your back will bring your hands back a fraction of an inch, close your legs more firmly on the horse and push your seat a little farther forward than his back takes it. Almost always you should tighten the left side of your back as the horse's body swings to the right and vice versa. Bracing your whole back at once is a form of punishment.

A supple, controllable back is very important and there are exercises that will help improve your body control. Any that stretch your back, such as sit-ups or bending over to touch your toes, will help supple your back. Knee bends help if you tuck your buttocks and exhale as you rise. Two more are done lying on your back with your knees bent, feet flat on the floor and your arms by your sides:

(1) Bring your legs with knees bent up and over your shoulders.

(2) With knees bent and feet on the floor bring your shoulders and upper body as far forward as possible. Always do all these exercises slowly, stretching your back muscles and holding that position for the count of four. Never do more than twelve of each at a time.

You can do mounted exercises and practice your seat in the longeing pen. Use side reins and have someone longe you, or tie your bridle reins in a knot and lay them on the horse's neck as you ride. (This can also be done in an arena with a well-trained horse.) Riding without stirrups is the best way to develop your seat, but be sure you do not hang on with your legs. It is legal to hang onto the pommel while getting your balance.

Start in the walk to practice keeping your position while staying relaxed. Then go to the trot with intermittent walk to regain your position until you can

Kathy Hansen and Apache. Mounted exercises on a reliable horse develop
the rider's seat, suppleness and confidence.

do it all in the trot. If being longed, be sure your
helper keeps the horse bent properly so the horse
does not displace you. Remember that on the circle
you maintain the outside leg, keep weight on both
seatbones and stretch the inside leg down without
leaning your upper body. In all exercises keep your
seat and legs in their proper positions.

Mounted exercises improve your riding posture,
balance, suppleness and relaxation. Suppling exercises consist of turning in the waist with arms out-
stretched and chest raised, and bending forward
from the hips to lie on the horse's neck, either
straight forward or reaching down either side.

To relax your shoulders and improve your posture

rotate them separately forward, up, back, and let
them drop into place relaxed.

Practice riding with your toes up without gripping
with your legs. To relax your ankles rotate your feet
separately or together, down, out, up and in. Do
this in a relaxed way, not as if your joints need
oiling. I sometimes just drop my toe and wiggle my
foot around to loosen my ankle.

You can make up your own exercises along these
lines. In all cases let your weight down in the saddle
and let the insides of your upper calves rest on the
horse's sides. This improves your balance and seat
while you are improving your posture, suppleness
and relaxation with the exercises.

6

AIDS AND INITIAL TRAINING

Some of you may be starting colts, so I feel I should briefly mention the best way to mount one before continuing this riding instruction. *Be sure the colt is under control.* The most secure way is to tie him with a strong halter and tie rope (no snap) to a sturdy post in a safe place—a corral fence of heavy poles or solid, 2-inch planks is good. Tie with about eighteen inches of tie rope between the halter and the post at wither height.

The steps in mounting are: (1) pull on the saddle from one side and then the other to get the colt used to the cinch binding; (2) with just your toe in the stirrup, put a little weight in the stirrup; (3) step up so you are standing in the stirrup and balanced over the horse's withers; (4) pet the colt on the off side; (5) wave your hand across his hips slowly; and (6) swing your leg slowly across, clearing his hips, and sit down gently. Each of these steps should be repeated until the colt accepts it before going on to the next.

When seated on the colt, pet him on both sides and on top of his hips. Let your legs rest on him; rub them on him; wiggle around gently in the saddle. Do all the mounting steps from the off side, too. Let him see what you are doing at all times and talk to him in a matter-of-fact way during it all. *As long as a colt knows you are there and is not given cause for alarm by sudden movements, he hardly ever will object to being mounted in this way. If he does move around some, it is because he must catch his balance. Reassure him.*

The best way to start riding a colt is on the longe, gradually getting him used to carrying your weight and then gradually taking over the control from the person longeing. If you do not have a reliable person to ride or longe him, then it is safest to ride him in a good corral or paddock no larger than sixty feet or smaller than fifty feet each way. Riding should be done on a circle to start with and just the way I will soon describe for all horses.

The other bit of knowledge all of you need is how to carry and use a whip. All horses, once relaxed, need to be encouraged to go forward just a little better than they want to. While the aids are your language for communicating with the horse, he usually will not understand at first. Stronger aids just will not do it, because trying to "squeeze" harder will just make you contort yourself out of position and so become ineffective. What is needed is an interpreter to help the horse understand your language.

The whip is the proper tool to use for this; and, properly used, it does not have to become a permanent accessory. It is not an instrument of punishment except in rare cases after the horse fully understands your language. Then one smart swat is all that is needed to remind the horse to be obedient. *Obedience is achieved by moving the horse forward, physically and mentally; and that is what you are telling him with the whip.*

Hold the whip in your hand along with the rein and hold it at its balance point. On a 4-foot whip this is usually about six inches down from the butt end. It is not necessary to grip it tightly. The whip is usually carried on the inside to aid your driving leg. To change it over as you change rein (direction), you take both reins in your whip hand, reach the other hand over and grasp the whip thumb down. The "new" whip hand takes it up and over into position. You then can take the rein back in that hand. To be able to do this and maintain even contact on the bit at the same time requires a lot of practice.

To acquaint the horse with the whip and to get the feel of it yourself, sit relaxed on your halted horse. Now move the tip end of the whip until you feel it touch the horse low on his body or thigh. You may need to bring that hand out to the side at first, and you probably will have to look for a time or two until you get the feel of the tip touching him.

Now, with the tip touching the horse and without using any aids, wiggle it to ask him to move. If he doesn't move, tap him lightly. If that doesn't move him, make each individual tap progressively harder until he does walk forward. As he walks forward, take the whip slightly off him. After a few steps, put it on him again to see if he will respond, tapping if necessary and removing it when he does walk forward better.

Once you both have the feel, you always use the whip at the same time you use your leg on that side—usually the inside. First you aid without it gently but firmly. No response? Aid again just the same and touch him with the whip at the same time. If necessary, do it again, tapping harder. *Always relax an aid and apply it again if needed. Never aid continuously. Aid in rhythm with the horse's rhythm or in the rhythm you desire. Always aid in the above order, getting progressively "louder" if needed, so the horse will learn to respond to aids that firmly whisper instead of needing a zap of the whip forever more.*

In order to avoid overuse of the whip, learn to ride so you are softly driving the horse every stride. All that is needed, as long as the horse is going forward willingly, is to sit tall with your stomach

Grasp the whip this way and it will be in the proper place in your hand when you take it up and over to the other side.

loose so you are relaxed in the waist. To get the feel of this and to be able to do it easily, practice riding in the walk. Just sitting relaxed, you will find that your pelvic area will work forward and back so your seat can follow the motion of the horse's back. Notice that this is actually one side of your seat and then the other—not both together. Try tightening your back muscles and feel your horse slow down. Just being relaxed in the waist encourages the horse to go forward.

All driving aids are pushing just a little farther than the horse's motion takes you. While tightening your back muscles will slow the horse down, tightening them

properly will make him move better. When his motion takes your left seatbone forward, his body will be swinging to the right and his left hind leg will be coming forward. As this happens, tighten the muscles on the left side of your back to push the left side of your pelvis forward as you close your left leg. Relax your left side and do the same with your right on the next stride as his body swings to the left.

Aid in rhythm with the horse. Start the driving aid when your seat is partly forward and flow into pushing just a little farther forward than the horse takes your seatbone. Do not try to use force because that destroys the effectiveness of your drive. Also, avoid pushing your seat from side to side. That slows the horse almost as much as a stiff back. Get the feel and gradually develop your body control until you can push easily. This is how you drive the horse forward in the walk.

In the trot, remember, you swing your hips forward as the horse pushes you up, and you relax to sit without leaning forward or pushing your seat to the rear. So just posting properly will keep the horse moving fairly well. If your shoulders go up and down as you post, you're straightening your knees and posting from your stirrups. If your lower legs swing, you're in the chair position and will pull on the reins to rise. Both of these mistakes slow the horse down, so correct them.

If the horse gets sluggish, follow through by pushing a little farther than his rhythm dictates. Flow into this push just the same as in the walk, except in posting you can drive only each time you sit, and going straight you drive with both seatbones at the same time. Stretch your legs down as you drive. In going around corners and on circles, drive more with your inside seat and leg than with your outside. This, combined with an outside leg, positions your inside hip farther forward making your hips parallel with horse's hips the way they should be. Your shoulders should be parallel with his shoulders, causing you to yield slightly on the outside rein without losing contact.

The basic principle of all riding is to ride the horse forward from the rear onto the bit. Never ride from the bit back, that is, pull on the reins to stop, slow or collect the horse. The horse's engine is in the rear and it must be engaged to make him maneuverable. If you keep this basic principle in mind at all times, you can avoid a lot of troubles and also avoid overuse of the reins. The things you must teach your horse for best results are those I already mentioned concerning longeing—go forward willingly under control, rhythmic, relaxed, straight and balanced. These are all taught gradually and in proper order.

Of the first four basics just mentioned, the one

that will probably give you the most problems is getting the horse to go straight. Anyone who has ever tried to ride a horse from one place to the next only to have him bend his body out and take the longest way around knows the frustration of a crooked horse. He simply is not controllable. But what is not obvious is that *he will never learn to go straight if you try to do it with the reins.* One of my favorite true-false questions that I give my students is, "Serpentines are useful because we can't make our horses go straight." False, of course, but true that we get "serpentines" when we try to straighten our horses with the reins. All good things come from the rear.

Theoretically, if you take equal contact with each rein and push forward equally with both seatbones, the horse will go on a straight line. It is a good idea to accept this as gospel so you will avoid the temptation to use your hands to correct the horse. So, *when the horse veers off the track for any reason, simply maintain the equal contact and drive him forward.* Notice that I told *you* to maintain the equal contact. No horse will seek contact himself for the first weeks of training. This means that every time he drops contact on either side, you have to swing that arm back from the shoulder to take the contact yourself. Do it smoothly so you do not jerk him. Then take the kink out of his neck with the other hand as you yield the first one forward without losing the contact you just took. Keep him moving forward as you do all this.

Now, you cannot go on a straight track forever, so let us turn a corner. Remember that the horse is straight going around a corner—or on a circle—when his spine is bent full length to the arc. So, without moving your inside hand back, you use the indirect rein there to indicate the direction, the outside leg to hold his haunches in, your outside shoulder slightly forward to yield without loss of contact so he can stretch outside, and the inside leg driving through the use of your back.

While weight is a factor in turning the horse, it is

Author and Iam. A bad corner is the fault of the rider. The horse is counterbent and falling on his inside shoulder because my outside shoulder is back, I have not flexed him with an inside indirect rein, and I am totally tense.

Don Mackay and Saltation. A good corner. Don is relaxed and in balance with the horse in every way so the horse is bending through the corner in rhythm and relaxation.

better not to think of it. Instead, look ahead where you are going to go by turning your whole upper body. This automatically yields the outside rein the amount needed for the corner you are turning. If you lean your upper body to the inside, you will take too much weight off the outside seatbone and the horse will turn too sharply. He will also turn too soon if you try to turn him with the inside rein and/or drop the outside contact.

Start your request for a corner about twenty feet ahead—ten feet in the walk—putting it together in the order named and then driving with your inside hip. Flow into all these aids so you do not assault the horse with them. *If your aids flow, then he can flow into the necessary changes; helping both of you to maintain your physical and mental equilibrium.*

You should ride in the forward position for quite some time to be in balance with the horse and to disturb him the least amount possible. Training starts on a large circle fifty to sixty feet in diameter. This helps control the rushing horse and the colt. *Remember that a circle is just a continued corner, so maintain your aids for a corner all the time you are on a circle.* If the horse makes the circle too small, avoid the temptation to guide him out with the reins. Instead, drive with your inside leg and hip, using the whip as needed. Make sure that you are not leaning in and that you are maintaining that outside contact. If he wants to go straight off the circle, use the leading rein momentarily to coax him in—but *never, never pull on that inside rein to make him turn.*

The first thing you must develop in the horse is rhythm. I know, I just spent paragraphs telling you how to get a horse straight, but this was to get you to stop riding the one quarter you can see and start riding the three quarters you can feel. Go on the large circle, take firm but elastic contact with the horse's mouth, maintain your aids for turning and trot the horse forward. If your hands bounce during posting, put them right down on the horse's neck on either side and just in front of his withers and *leave them there.* You can very easily squeeze your hands

shut or relax them and can turn your inside wrist while your hands stay on his neck.

While the circle helps control the horse, you cannot let the excitable one go storming around like a maniac. Take firm contact; clench your fists and immediately start to relax them, clenching and relaxing them again and again the amount needed to establish a rhythm. On the other hand, if your horse is sluggish, still maintain contact and drive him forward—at first just to get him moving and then, in order to establish rhythm, each time he starts to slow down.

This initial rhythm will probably be rushy in both cases. Often when the rhythm is established, the horse automatically drops into the relaxed, longer strides. If he continues to rush, you can help him slow his rhythm by slowing your posting, rising barely off the saddle and staying down just slightly longer than his rhythm dictates. In order to establish rhythm with relaxation you must feel the horse so you can use your hands, legs and rhythm at the appropriate times with the appropriate amounts of firmness. *You want the same relaxed, working rhythm that you got on the longe, so keep this ticking away in your head and work to keep him in it until it becomes habit.*

The other thing you want to develop now is the horse's stretching his head down just as you have him doing on the longe. One reason you want this is to teach him to seek contact with the bit. The other reason you want him stretching down is to stretch his whole top line so he can stride under with his hind feet and eventually bring his whole forehand up without dropping his back. When a horse travels consistently with lowered head (neck about parallel with ground or just slightly higher) and striding up onto the tracks of his front feet, and when his rhythm is slow and even, he can start swinging his back. The swinging back makes your ride more comfortable besides making the horse's work easier for him.

When he is stepping under well, relaxed and

Shirley McCarthy and Misty. In initial training yield forward when the horse lowers its head this way. This helps the horse accept the bit and seek contact.

rhythmic, he should start stretching down. Watch carefully for this so that every time he offers the least bit to lower his head, you can slide your hands forward along his neck to accommodate him—but without losing contact. This tells him that you will not restrain him from seeking contact with the bit. As you keep him moving forward in relaxed rhythm, his head will come back up some. Slide your hands back as his head comes up so you maintain the contact. *If you yield when he stretches, maintaining elastic contact wherever his head is, he will soon want to keep the contact himself with his neck about parallel to the*

ground. That is how he is most comfortable at this time.

As soon as he is working well on the circle, trot right on down the track of the full arena trying to maintain the whole performance you have just developed. Ride corners carefully and on the same large arc as your circle. If he starts rushing badly, go immediately on a circle wherever you are and reestablish the rhythm, relaxation and lowered head. Then try again to go large (full arena).

When you have trotted him for about ten minutes and gotten him at least rhythmic and relaxed (head

69

Author and Iam. Perfection in initial training: Iam is rhythmic, relaxed, striding under, yielded to the bit, bent to the large circle and carrying his head at the proper level. My toe should be pointed straight ahead, otherwise the outside leg is good.

lowered, too, if possible), bring him quietly down to a walk. To do this bring yourself up straighter and let your weight down into the saddle. Brace your back (stop its motion) one side and then the other as you fix the corresponding hand (squeeze your fist shut and clamp your elbow against your body). Do this *with* the horse's rhythm, not against it. As he starts to take the walk, start riding the walk yourself, maintaining contact. After several strides of a good walk, feed the reins through your fingers to lengthen them and invite him to stretch down. This will eventually lead to his "chewing the reins out of your

hands"—which I will soon explain. Keep him walking forward well.

After a minute of free walk this way, quietly gather up the reins to trotting length; walk him in a change of direction and do all this same work on the other rein. Always work equally on both reins (directions). If he offers to canter during any of this work, let him canter on for a few strides. Go on a circle to control him. If it is a colt that might buck in the canter, discourage it by refusing to break your posting rhythm when you feel him want to canter. I once did this with my colt all around the arena at

Kathy Hansen and Apache. The free walk on a loose rein. When the horse stretches down this way in the free walk, the work has been correct. Ask him to yield in the walk before feeding the reins out gradually to loose reins.

least twice. I was beginning to think he was lame because he tried to hop into the canter every other stride the whole time. He finally settled into the trot and was okay, but he sure had me worried for a little while there!

I guess we had better bring this horse to a halt now, otherwise you'll be like the hard and fast roper that dabbed his loop on a puma. They say he's still galloping around the mountains trying to outrun that big cat! To ask for the halt let all your weight right down onto his back so you feel yourself get heavier. Leave your legs relaxed, brace your back and fix your hands alternately in rhythm with the horse's body swing. Help out by saying "Ho-ho," letting your voice drop on the end as you brace on the fourth stride to come to the halt immobile. Later on you'll be able to drive him onto the bit to halt him, but at this stage he would just lose his balance and keep walking.

There are two other things I want to say at this time:

(1) Praise your horse often for doing what you want, but examine your riding carefully when you fail to get what you ask. Dressage's motto—the

Author and Pi Dough. Doubling a horse right back on himself this way is an excellent
safety measure against bucking and running away. Be sure to drop outside contact and to move the
horse forward and take contact as he comes out of the turn.

horse can do no wrong, only the rider.

(2) It seems that all of us self-taught dressage riders end up with runaway horses. I think this is because of all this necessary preaching about do-nothing hands and sympathetic riding. Eventually we learn that when a horse throws his head in the air and charges off, it is a gross disobedience that requires gross control. The moment a horse does this, drop your outside contact and pull him right back on himself with the other rein. Keep your doubling hand low and a little out to the side. After this you can immediately and calmly return to the sympathetic riding and training.

7

DEVELOPING THE FOUNDATION

Things can look so easy on paper and be so hard to do. This is especially true of riding and training a horse. As I sit here at my typewriter I can see in my mind and feel in my body all the things I am telling you. But I wonder what visions and feelings my words convey to you. Since the biggest part of my knowledge has come through observation and feel rather than instruction alone, I wonder how to let you know what is right and what is wrong with what you are doing from this instruction. Remember that you must have feel of your horse; and in order to have feel, you must be relaxed. But how do you know whether what you feel is right or wrong?

Did you ever notice at a horse show how lots of horses make you tense up to help ride them through their performances? Then comes a horse that lets you just sit back and enjoy the performance. I think you can take it as a very sound rule: if you do not have to help ride the horse, it is a good performance.

I am sure you can apply this same thing to your riding. When it feels so good you no longer feel you have to strain to help your horse do it, then he is doing it right. When he dawdles along in an unanimated jog, your body will be trying to make sure he takes the next step and the next. When he goes rushing forward as if going to a fire, your body will be up-tight trying to keep up with him. But when he goes forward willingly with rhythm and relaxation, your whole self will say, "Oh, what a relief!" and go along with him easily. And guess what—your horse is saying, "Oh, what a relief! My rider finally got it put together!" *Know the mechanics. Search for the feel.*

It is easy to sit here and tell you step-by-step how to train a horse just as if everything will go smoothly. Actual practice shows that it does not work that way. Circles are perfectly round things, but most horses do not seem to know that. They veer out on the side near the barn and cut in on the side away from it. They go on small circles when you want large ones. Enrolling them in a plane geometry class just won't help. Check up to make sure you're maintaining outside contact at all times. That you're not leaning in with your upper body. That you're keeping your inside hand turned and your outside leg in position. And stop correcting your horse with the reins!

When he makes the circle too small or cuts in, drive more with your inside leg, using the whip as needed. When he skids out, use your outside leg by rolling or tapping your heel in rhythm with his stride. If he still skids out, put the whip on the outside for awhile and use it at the same time you use that heel.

If your horse hasn't started stretching his head down, it may be that your contact isn't firm enough. I find "western" riders very reluctant to take good contact. They've lived with this loose-rein myth for so long, they think contact is synonymous with rough hands. If the contact comes and goes, which it does with loose reins, the horse will be so worried

about where the bit will be next that he'll be afraid to stretch down. Good hands hold the reins firmly with elastically closed fists and keep reliable contact with the horse's mouth. The fists are squeezed shut tightly only when using a fixed hand briefly. They are wide open when the ring fingers have moved out from the palms no more than an inch. Thumbs and forefingers never open but are relaxed, except when the hands are fixed.

If you are maintaining good contact, you can help encourage a horse to stretch down by smoothly rolling the inside hand toward your body and then unrolling it. It's rhythmic, taking about two trot strides to roll in and about two to roll out—out to the indirect rein if you're on the circle, out to the direct rein if you're going straight. Be sure to yield forward with both hands when he does start to stretch. If you have missed the boat on this, you have discouraged him from trying.

You can help him establish the stretching down in his mind in this way—each time he stretches down, while he's still down and your hands are forward, let your weight down to coax him to walk. As he takes the walk, feed the reins out through your fingers and walk him on a loose rein. Once around the circle walking, then carefully gather up the reins so you don't startle him; ease him into the trot; and do it again. This reward system quickly teaches most horses to stretch down everytime asked. Soon you can keep on trotting and his head will come back up to just where you want it with his neck just slightly above parallel to the ground.

When the horse will work most of the time in this position and will stretch down when asked, it is time to start limiting how far down he goes and to ask him to yield more to the bit. The work you have been doing teaches him to yield (relax his jaw), but now you can ask a little more of him. In riding it is the same principle as on the longe. The outside rein tells the horse how far he can stretch. The inside indirect rein asks for the yield just as the longe line did. If you asked with a direct rein, the horse could bore into the bit forever more. The indirect rein flexes his head slightly to the inside making it easier for him to relax any resistance in his neck. The outside contact must be a constant length but elastic through elastic fingers, and the horse must be kept moving forward in relaxed, energetic rhythm.

Start each lesson by getting your horse going rhythmic and relaxed, stretching down and coming back up to the proper position. Then start giving him a place to reach the bit by no longer moving your hands forward. Maintain equal contact and go on a trotting circle so that you are using an inside indirect rein. When he wants to stretch down, simply maintain that same length of rein, no longer moving your hands forward to accommodate him.

Do not think for a minute that you take back on the reins to get him to yield. That would be setting his head, a thing we never do.

If, instead of yielding, he bores into the bit, keep him moving energetically and ask him to yield by rhythmically using your inside hand the same way you asked him to stretch down. We want him to stretch into the bit and yield because he reached it—not because we pulled it back. When he does yield, he will duck his head slightly, bringing his nose back. *The contact will get light. Leave it that way. That is what you want.*

Almost immediately he may stretch his nose out again, either because he loses his balance or because you move your hands forward some. Ask him again

Author and Iam. A colt raises his head because he is resistant or has lost his balance. Move him forward onto the bit. Pulling on the reins to control a horse will develop that bulge on the underneath side of his neck permanently.

His balance regained, Iam yields to the bit. Notice how the shape of his neck has changed. Even a naturally ewe-necked horse will develop a pretty neck if ridden properly.

to yield. Do this over and over within this long framework until he learns that you want him to stay yielded. Remember, you will get it gradually, not through force. You can encourage his yielding just as you did his stretching, by coaxing him down to the walk while yielded. His nose may go forward as he takes the walk. Do not move your hands forward; just ask again for the yield and as he does, feed the reins through your fingers for the walk on loose reins. Then do the work again after a circle of rewarding walk.

When he yields on the circle, you can go large and get the yield at every corner. Then you can also ask going straight by rolling your inside hand into the indirect position and relaxing it to the direct rein. *He will gradually learn to stay yielded if, as he yields, you do not move your hands back to maintain the firm contact you started with. That would punish him*

for yielding. Do not move them forward, either, since that would tell him you did not really mean it. Firm contact feels fairly heavy on your hands. Light contact (which must come from the horse's yielding at this time) gives you the feel that you have something in your hands but no weight. No contact feels empty in your hands.

Again, I am going to talk about straightness even though this is the next to the last thing you will get with your horse. This straightness has to do with contact—the thing you are developing as you do this other work. The horse must learn to seek contact himself so he will stretch into the bit whenever you yield the reins. I have already told you to maintain the contact yourself at this stage of training. Maybe you noticed that this made the horse cockeyed at times.

The horse has what is called a stiff side and a

With flexible contact ride the horse forward to the bit to train him to go straight. Note the lightness of the contact—the horse's doing, and I left it that way.

hollow side. On the hollow side he will not want to go up to the bit (allow contact). On the stiff side he will not want to yield. When you take equal contact, he will probably want to stay bent in his neck. Simply maintain the contact, ignore the improper bend and ride him on. When you feel him relax, you can then straighten his neck by taking with the hand on the stiff side as you yield softly with the other. *This must be done by feel, not force, just as all riding is done by feel. Permanent results come about gradually.*

Another thing you need to know is that a horse is narrower at the shoulders than at the hips. If you are riding inside a fenced arena, almost all young horses tend to go with their shoulders the same distance from the fence as their hips. This, of course, means that they are not straight—a straight horse steps the hind foot into the track of the corresponding front

foot. Do not try to force or guide the horse's shoulder away from the fence. *Simply encourage the horse to step a little more forward with his inside hind leg and stretch a little more into the outside rein by driving him forward more with your inside leg. This will bring about a gradual improvement.*

So far I have given you only two figures to ride, the circle and the full arena. This is quite sufficient while you are establishing the rhythm and lowered head, but now you need to go on to others to help supple the horse and to keep up his interest.

In the diagrams you'll find (1) change of rein, (2) change out of the circle, (3) flat serpentine. Change of rein and change out of the circle can be used early in each lesson, but the flat serpentine should be used toward the end of the lesson when everything feels just right. Use these figures often and in varied order to avoid a routine. Try to avoid staying too long on a circle and on the same rein going large once you have established the rhythm and lowered head at the beginning of each ride. Work equally on both reins, but do it alternately rather than all on one rein followed by all on the other.

Figures are not to be taken lightly. Every one is an exercise in bending and straightening the horse. You are not just training a horse to bend because you are turning him but to turn because you bend him. Watch a horse walking around loose. When his head goes to the left, his body bows out to the right; therefore, if you can control the bend and straightness of his body, you can control his direction of travel.

Every corner is an exercise in bending and should be ridden carefully. Trotting on the track to the right from K to H, prepare for the corner before reaching H by first putting your outside leg back and driving with your inside leg to start the horse bending in his body. Next apply the indirect rein inside to flex his head and then continue to drive him through the corner to maintain rhythm and energy. Before you are completely around the corner, start your aids back to normal position, then immediately prepare for the next corner.

How far ahead of the corner you start to prepare your horse depends upon his speed of travel and his responsiveness. On a green horse you would have to prepare sooner; on any horse you would prepare sooner in the trot and canter than in the walk. Also, the green horse cannot bend as much as the trained horse, so his early corners would have to be long without the straightening at C and A. Gradually he can bend more and so make each corner on a smaller arc. The important things are to prepare the horse before he must turn or straighten so he is able to maintain his balance and rhythm while changing, and to use your aids firmly but not suddenly so there is no doubt in his mind what you are asking of him.

The change of rein is the easiest figure for the

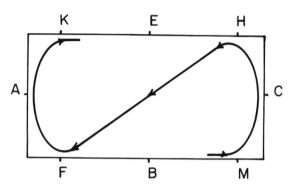

horse. After riding the short side, continue the corner at H until you have started toward X. You should start straightening the horse before you are actually aimed at X because it takes him a little while to unbend. Aim through X toward a point on the B side of F so you can start bending the horse before reaching the track and have him finish his corner onto it at F and continue on around the corner. The change of rein can be started at either end, going on either hand, but always after riding through the short side of the arena (the end of it).

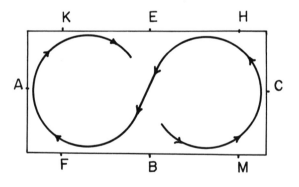

The change out of the circle is more difficult than the change of rein because there is less straight distance between the changes of direction. While it looks like a figure eight, it is different because you are changing direction and so will stay on the new circle until another change is wanted. To ride this

78

change you must start asking for the opposite bend as you approach the middle, where the horse should take one or two straight strides. If you ask smoothly, he will take those straight strides as he goes through the process of changing the bend of his body.

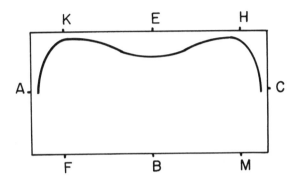

The flat serpentine should be ridden after the horse is limbered up and responsive. The object is to bend the horse from side to side to improve his responsiveness and suppleness. Change your aids smoothly as you approach each change of bend. This figure can be ridden on both long sides on either rein. At E and B you should be about four to six feet off the track.

All this is not as easy as it sounds. At first you want the horse to make all these changes with his head in its normal working position, neck about parallel to the ground. As work progresses you want him to learn to do all his work yielding to the bit. If you ask too abruptly, if he loses his balance or if you lose your balance, his head will fly up. Often he will decide for himself that you plan to go straight or continue on a circle or whatever—then he will need help with a leading rein.

You must work for gradual improvement. You must work sympathetically to get him to keep his rhythm, balance and carriage as consistently as possible. You must work to get him to flow from bent to straight to bent. Do not get impatient—just keep trying. Praise him as often as possible. Use your rhythm to maintain his; stay relaxed so you don't upset his balance; plan ahead

so your aids can flow. It's quite upsetting to the horse to be told at the last minute, "Oh! I meant to turn here."

When a horse is working yielded, his neck can get to feeling crampy even in this present long framework. After about five minutes of work, he will need a chance to stretch his muscles. Ask him down to a walk. Walk a few strides with contact to establish the walking rhythm and his yielding to the bit, then feed the reins through your fingers slowly and steadily to invite him to stretch his head down. When it is fully stretched down and he is walking without rushing, let him have loose rein. Do not stop your own work just because the horse gets a rest. Keep him walking forward well.

When the horse is working correctly, he begins to chew the bit. This is working his tongue under the bit much as if he is licking his lips. He should also get foam in his mouth—the more the better. When the work has

This foam in the horse's mouth indicates the horse is relaxed and working on contact.

Kathy Hansen and Watirah. The long, relaxed canter wanted at this stage of training. At this point in canter bound, a light half-halt occurs when the horse is ridden on contact. A stronger half-halt (more push with the pelvis on briefly fixed hands) will cause the horse to balance more to the rear and bound higher.

been correct so he is starting to chew the bit, and after a few strides of walk you invite him to stretch down by opening your fingers gradually, he should *"chew the reins out of your hands."* He does not jerk them; *he just chews them down and down and down and down in rhythm with his walk.* Always walk on a few strides before opening your fingers so he will not object later on when you keep the contact and continue work. Do not just throw the reins away when you come down to the free walk. He cannot learn to chew them out of your hands if you have already dropped them.

Along with these figures, you also want to start walk-trot transitions toward the end of most lessons. Ask for the walk when he is trotting correctly, and the trot when he is walking correctly. Aim for five strides walk, ten trot, five walk, etc., all done without his flinging his head up. It must come gradually. Do not let the reins go loose when doing this work; that would make him lose his balance. *Slightly firmer contact and firmer closing of your legs during the transition will help him keep his balance.* The transitions start him shifting his balance toward the rear without your doing anything else about it.

Vicki Navarra and Mission Ridge. The long canter on contact just going into the half-halt. Note the horse's face nearly in the vertical.

Cantering is introduced to the horse on the large circle. Besides using the circle to help control the horse, you have the aids for the proper lead already in effect. It is natural for the horse to take the left lead when turning to the left, and vice versa; therefore, you do not usually have trouble getting the proper lead when he stays bent to the circle as he makes the transition. In this way you use his natural inclination while you teach him your language: your canter aids. The canter we are talking about is really a controlled gallop, not the canter you see in the show ring; but I prefer to use the term "canter" for

this so you do not get the mental picture of speed.

When first riding the canter, you should take the forward position to give the horse as much freedom as possible to use his back. Your knees and ankles will take up the shock of any awkwardness on his part. When this basic canter (controlled gallop) is established and you can relax down into the saddle, you will find that the horse's back brings your seat forward and then back. To ride the canter correctly you should have both the appearance and feel that your whole body, right down to your seatbones, is swinging from your shoulders forward and relax,

The point in the canter bound when the rider's seat is in the relaxed back position just ready to start forward. Study all three photos to see how the rider's body swings forward and back as though pivoted at the shoulders.

forward and relax, while your shoulders travel in a straight line. Your hands must follow his head motion without loss of contact, and your outside leg stays in the outside position, even when going large. Do not try to keep your legs stationary; when they are relaxed and on the horse, they will have some motion corresponding to his motion.

The aids for a left lead are just the same as the aids for a left corner or circle with just two more requests added to get the canter. So first get your horse working, relaxed and rhythmic, in the trot on the large circle, properly bent to it. Your first request that you add to the aids already in effect is "Prepare to canter." To prepare to canter, a horse

must be balanced toward the rear even though at this time it will be only slightly. You express this request by driving slightly more on the sit-stride as you momentarily fix your outside hand. This is called a half-halt on the outside rein.

The half-halt is a very useful tool. In Disney's "Miracle of the White Stallions," when they start working the horses for the exhibition for Patton, Podhajsky comes down the center line in the canter and starts a canter pirouette. This is similar to a rollback or spin except the horse must keep the distinct canter beat as he makes the turn on the haunches. On the first stride of Podhajsky's pirouette, you catch your breath because the horse has fallen forward (lost his collection) and you swear he will never make it on around. But Podhajsky puts him together with a half-halt and completes the movement beautifully.

The half-halt can be used in varying degrees according to what the horse is doing, what you want him to do and what he is capable of doing at the time. It is used to balance the horse during a movement, and so warn him of a change of direction, gait or "speed." It is used to get his attention when he is distracted from his work. *You always half-halt by driving onto fixed hands—never by simply taking on the reins.*

Back to "prepare to canter." You are riding a green horse that cannot balance too much, so half-halt lightly each sit-stride. This should not speed up your horse's rhythm but should make him feel to you that he is able to make a change of gait. Then you ask for the canter on the next sit-stride by stretching your inside leg down as you push more with your inside seatbone and soften your hands. If your horse seems to have trouble making the transition, try simply driving rhythmically each sit-stride until he finally does make the change. A sluggish horse may need a tap with the whip as you ask. If so, start with an easy tap as you drive, tapping a little harder each time until he does canter. Using the whip on his inside shoulder instead of on his body can avoid his bucking, but hitting a horse suddenly and hard anywhere can cause him to buck going into the canter.

If your horse simply rushes off in the trot instead of taking the canter, you may have softened your hands too soon or dropped contact altogether. Some horses, especially colts, just cannot carry themselves well enough yet and need more work trotting forward yielded to the bit. If the horse takes the wrong lead, you probably dropped contact and let him unbend. Keep him bent but do not over-bend him with your efforts. The bend is to the left for a left lead and to the right for a right lead.

In all this work be patient. Do not punish him for mistakes and do not punish him by over-aiding (using the aids too harshly). Your goal is a calm transition every time; therefore anything that causes him excitement now would start a problem. When things go wrong, quietly bring the horse back to the relaxed, rhythmic trot and try again.

Work for long, rhythmic, relaxed strides in the canter, using your body motion to push a little farther forward than the horse dictates. When he is cantering this way on the circle, go off the circle around the arena keeping your rhythm to help him keep his same relaxed rhythm. Work for easy transitions to the canter.

The aids for a designated lead when going straight are the same as when going on the circle or through a corner. Flex the horse with an indirect inside rein and an outside leg, half-halt on the outside rein, then push the horse into the canter with your inside leg. The only difference is that you do not flex the horse as much going straight as you would on the circle or in the corner. Flex him to the right for a right lead and to the left for a left lead. If you are always definite and consistent with your canter aids, first on the circle and then in corners, the horse will learn to take the proper lead on the same aids when going straight. Ask for smooth transitions down to the trot by driving with an inside braced back onto an outside fixed rein. Follow this immediately by starting to ride the trot. This breaks up his canter rhythm and prevents his leaning on the reins.

When the canter is long, rhythmic and relaxed and the transitions are smooth, you can begin doing canter-trot transitions to start the horse's balancing toward the rear. Start this work on the circle, gradually getting the transitions down to ten beats of trot and ten canter bounds for about three or four times each. Work equally both directions, giving the horse 1-minute periods of free walk in between.

8

WALK AND TROT CAVALLETTI— RIDING OUT

I do not think there is anything that can take the place of cavalletti work in the training of a horse. It can help lower the horse's head, even his rhythm, develop his balance and impulsion, and lengthen or shorten his stride. It is a must in preparing a horse to jump, but we will get into that phase of it later. This work is also a big help in developing the rider's seat.

A convenient length for cavalletti poles is four to six feet. They should be fairly smooth logs six to eight inches in diameter or 4-inch poles nailed onto blocks to make them six to eight inches from the top to the ground. If you already have regular jump rails, you might want to construct several pairs of box ends that make it convenient for you to use your rails for all phases of cavalletti work, including jumping.

To construct each box, make a framework of 2-by-4's 2-feet square, and cut a 2-foot square of quarter-inch plywood for each side of this frame. In one corner of each plywood face cut an oversized

The construction of the box ends, here set at canter cavalletti height with an X-fence beyond.

4-inch square hole to slip the rail through. It should be spaced four inches from one edge of the plywood and eight inches from the adjacent edge. Remember that you have a left and a right face so get the two holes lined up when you nail these pieces on your frame.

This gives you a square box about four inches thick with the hole for the rail situated so you can get an 8-inch height for trot work and a 16-inch and 20-inch height for canter work. Simply turn the boxes to whichever height you need. You can stand them on top of each other to get more height and can store them easily when not in use.

You can set up your cavalletti in an area of their own or just inside the track in the arena. The footing should not be hard as that would work a hardship on the horse's feet and legs, and it should not be slick in wet weather. If using the logs, imbed them slightly in the soft footing or block them on each side with a few small rocks so they will not roll.

Walk cavalletti are spaced 2'4" apart for most of our horses, and up to 2'10" for horses over 16 hands. Trot poles are set up four feet apart and can go out to 4'6". We will deal with the spacing of canter poles later on. Do not trot your horse over walk poles or walk him over trot poles as this would defeat the purpose of the exercises. If he can walk and trot and canter over cavalletti properly spaced for each respective gait, he certainly can pick his way over slash and rocks and through brush at a walk—which is the sensible way to do it if the stuff is thick.

Cavalletti work can start as soon as the horse trots forward, rhythmic and relaxed. He does not have to be yielding to the bit yet but really should not be going with high head and hollow back. However, a horse that finds difficulty in stretching his head down can be helped with work over the poles if it is done sympathetically. Always do enough flat work to warm up your horse before doing cavalletti work, to avoid damaging his muscles and tendons.

Most horses will walk across four poles right from the beginning, especially if you have done the cavalletti work with them on the longe. If your horse does not walk freely across the four, start with just one and add another daily. If you start right out with trot poles, it's a must that you start with just one or with two singles—one on each side of the arena. The next day you can space two together and so on up to four. Some horses will quickly go up to three quite well, then blow it every time you add the fourth one. These horses either aren't strong enough or aren't balanced enough yet. Stick with three until your horse has developed enough and really enjoys the work. There isn't any value in using more than four cavalletti. It's strenuous work for the horse and four are quite sufficient to get any results you need.

When you plan to cross the cavalletti, always make your turn so you are headed straight for the middle of them. Don't turn on the track and then swerve to get in front of the poles, and don't swerve back to the track after crossing. (Crossing in the middle of a flat serpentine would be an exception.) As you approach, look straight ahead, maintain equal contact and steady rhythm. Don't try to guide him with the reins if he swerves to avoid the poles, but simply drive him on with quiet determination

and equal contact. Bring him right on around the arena and repeat until he goes where you're looking.

While you can ride across the walk cavalletti sitting in the normal, balanced position, you should always take the forward position and put your hands down on the horse's neck when starting him on the trot poles. Lots of horses feel they have to give a mighty shove with the hind legs, and you do not want to bang their backs and mouths. When you both get the feel of this exercise, you can change to the posting trot; and later on when he is swinging his back, you can use the sitting trot.

For cavalletti work to be effective, you have to maintain the horse's desire to go forward willingly under control, rhythmic and relaxed. Lots of horses slow down on approach; and while it is okay to let your horse do this initially, you should start driving rhythmically each stride when the horse is accustomed to crossing the poles. If he rushes on approach, still drive but slow your own rhythm to influence him to slow his. If he rushes leaving the poles, you may be banging his mouth and back or dropping contact—check up on it. When he goes across with relaxed rhythm, work to maintain that rhythm as you go on around the arena. If he offers to stretch his head down, yield with your arms and body to accommodate him without losing contact.

After the horse is well established at trotting straight across the poles, take advantage of the improvement in his way of going by going right off the poles to flat work, riding various figures while tactfully maintaining the improvement. When this starts to fall apart, go back to the cavalletti to get it again and then go on to flat work again. Take advantage of the improved balance to get better lateral bend by turning smoothly onto a nice half-circle immediately after the poles.

If your horse has a sluggish walk or choppy trot, you can improve these after he takes the poles easily. Widen the spacing for that gait about an inch daily up to the maximum (2'10" for the walk, 4'6" for the trot), and drive him forward rhythmically on

Author and Pi Dough. Taking the trot poles in the forward position with hands on the horse's neck to avoid bumping his back and mouth. Note how the horse uses himself.

the approach. Doing this more than four or five times each day may result in sore muscles for the horse. All cavalletti work is strenuous, so twenty minutes of concentrated work every other day is plenty—or about ten or fifteen times across each way mixed with flat work daily.

Cavalletti work improves the horse's performance because he must put more effort into it than just going on the flat. It develops his rhythm because the spacing is exact. It develops his relaxation and stretching down because that is the easiest way for him to do the exercise. It develops your seat because you have to learn to take the extra push by getting deeper into your knees.

You want rhythm and relaxation because no athlete can perform well with tense, jerky movements. You want the horse to stretch his head down because this stretches his back, making it supple and strong. This is a must for a horse with a low back and a high head, and it is desirable for all horses. You want the horse to travel with his neck nearly horizontal and stepping under, driving from behind, because this develops his engine (hindquarters) and starts his back swinging. All this leads to impulsion (spring in gaits) which you want so that he no longer pounds his feet and legs on the ground and you on his back. Finally, you want balance so the horse carries himself. Balance makes him light on

Here I post in the upright position and Pi Dough balances himself more to the rear. Pi Dough's thick neck prevents his keeping his face in the vertical, a thing which causes him discomfort in breathing.

the contact and in his movements.

All of these things supple the horse and make your riding easier and more pleasurable. All of them prevent fatigue in the horse and rider. I am sure that all endurance riders and horses could benefit from all basic dressage training, including cavalletti, simply because it would develop the muscles, suppleness and relaxation that are vital to preventing wear and tear and debilitating fatigue. I have seen winning endurance horses with plenty of muscle fore and aft but none on their backs. That back carries the weight and ties all motor activities together. No back, no *superior* performance.

You are probably quite frustrated by now with all this talk about arenas. Some of you may even have had a hard time finding a level spot large enough for longeing. I know how you feel, but count yourselves lucky if you have lots of hills to ride up and down. There is nothing that can beat hill climbing to develop a horse's hindquarters, back and balance, if you let him stretch down. I use longeing, arena work, cavalletti, and hill work because each supplements the others very nicely.

If you have a place to ride out on trails, plan on doing so as soon as you can control your horse. I have no patience with people who ride out on a green, green colt and just hope nothing bad happens. Not only is it dangerous, it is a good way to

89

Author and Pi Dough. A brisk but relaxed trot out on the trail relieves the monotony while continuing the training. Pi Dough can yield to the bit better and I should relax my elbows.

start some very bad habits that will take months to cure. Even if you do not have much room at home, you can find some area there where you can ride your horse safely while you teach him thoroughly to go and turn and stop so you can control him.

In riding out you will find places where you can work on a large circle and others where you can work on long lines. You may have brush to wind your way through and logs to step over. These latter you may be able to arrange for cavalletti. The important thing is to ride your horse every step of the way, asking him to bend properly on every turn and to relax into a rhythmic trot on every long trail. You do not have to ride in an arena to get your horse stretching down, yielding to the bit and making smooth transitions.

Long, gently sloping hills are excellent places to start cantering a colt since the hill will control him,

and you can urge him on to long, rhythmic strides. You can find a place somewhere to canter on the circle to educate him to the leads. Steeper hills help develop his balance. Lean forward and grab a handful of mane going up, giving him enough rein that he can bound up if he wants. Later on when he is stronger, he will be able to walk up steep hills, and you should ask him to do so.

The colt can walk down hills if you help him balance by leaning forward enough to be in balance with him, and push him onto the bit to get his hind feet under him. Keep flexible contact, softening it when you feel him get his own balance and firming it up again when he loses his balance and starts rushing.

You will both enjoy the trail work a lot, but *do work*—do not be just a tourist.

90

Make use of the brush to bend your horse around—here beautifully done.

Use your outside leg to bend the horse—but relax it and look ahead where you're going, not down at the horse like this.

9

SITTING TROT—
CHECKING HORSE'S
PROGRESS

When your horse starts swinging his back it is time to start riding the trot sitting, so I had better explain how it is done. In dressage tests, every trot above 2nd Level is ridden sitting. Western show riders are required to sit the trot, but English riders are required to post. So why should all of us learn to ride sitting? One reason is that it just plain looks better when it is done properly so the rider's seat stays glued to the saddle. Another reason is that it is often more comfortable than posting when the horse is moving properly.

While the above reasons might be sufficient, we find as we become more exacting in the standards of performance for our horses that we hunt for better ways to get that performance more easily. Sitting the trot, we can aid the horse more consistently, rhythmically and subtly. Being on the horse's back every trot stride instead of every other one, we can feel every move the horse makes and aid him every stride when necessary. This makes it easier to improve the horse's trot and to influence it toward a consistently better performance when it is improved.

I have read instructions for learning to sit that said, "All you have to do is stay relaxed and you will go with the horse and not bounce." It sounds great, but just try to relax on a horse that is jabbing you in the seat on every stride! That is an extreme; you really should post that kind, but even an easy mover will push you up some, causing you to stiffen and so prevent your staying down in the saddle.

The way to learn to ride so you become part of the horse is to establish first your correct posture and suppleness. If you have been doing the exercises faithfully, you should be getting supple and well on your way to standing, walking and sitting with a straight back—that is, each vertebra stacked neatly on top of the one below it. Think of your backbones as a bunch of building blocks that must be lined up perfectly true in order to keep them from toppling over. The thing that keeps them lined up is the development of the proper muscles, not tense effort on your part. So if you have neglected the exercises, look them up and get busy! They develop the proper muscles.

Besides doing the exercises regularly, practice correct posture at all times. When you sit anywhere including your car, sit up straight, scootch the bottom of your seat slightly forward and then relax. If sofas and overstuffed chairs do not permit you to do this comfortably, do not sit on them. When you walk, stand up straight, tuck your buttocks and relax. Then walk by swinging each hip forward without twisting from side to side, so you take long, relaxed strides just like your horse should take.

If you are inclined to be round-shouldered, rotate each shoulder forward, up, back and let it drop into place. Repeat this each time you feel your shoulders droop forward. Keep your eyes ahead with your head up but your chin in. Tuck it in and then relax; do not try to hold it there with tight muscles. Through such simple things as these repeated many times a

day, as well as doing the exercises, good posture and better riding ability become possible and habitual, not just something you force yourself into temporarily.

The best way to learn to ride sitting trot is on the longe on a horse that goes rhythmically forward with long strides and lowered head. Such a horse is swinging his back at least some and so is easier to sit. The rhythm is necessary so you can get the swing of it. If you cannot team up with a friend on longeing, you can put the side reins on your horse, knot the bridle reins so you can lay them on his neck and practice in your longeing pen—if you made one. Otherwise you will have to practice during regular riding.

During practice, you should ride without stirrups to help you stay down in the saddle. With the sport

Tie up the stirrups of the stock saddle this way. If you just let them hang to ride without stirrups, they will force your legs too far forward.

94

saddle you can cross the stirrups in front of the saddle out of your way. If you ride a stock saddle, turn the stirrups up to the front and tie them with the saddle strings or a cord looped around the horn. Position yourself in the saddle; let your legs hang relaxed; straighten your back so your pelvis is vertical; and then relax. During all your riding, reposition yourself in the saddle this way.

Start your practice in the walk to give yourself a chance to relax and go with the horse's movement. Pay close attention to the feel of the horse's back under you. Notice that it takes first one seatbone and then the other forward. As you get this feel and relax your stomach so your seat can go with this motion, follow through by pushing your pelvis slightly farther forward than the horse's back takes it. Be careful not to push from side to side—always the push is forward.

Now go into the trot, staying as relaxed as possible and feeling for this same alternating push of the horse's back. All you want to do at this time is relax everything without slumping, so the horse's movement can take your seatbones forward alternately on each stride. At this stage it helps some people to lean back as far as possible and keep the outside hand on the pommel of the saddle. Then each time you start to bounce you can use your hand to pull the front of the saddle up into your seat, immediately relaxing the pull to avoid tension.

Several things almost invariably happen when

Mary Alexander on Rena; Vicki Navarra longeing. Initially, leaning back can help the rider learn to sit the trot. Rena's strong trot helps keep Mary tense.

95

Now Mary is more relaxed and going with the horse better. Keep your head up and your chin in but relaxed. With more practice Mary's knees will lower.

you start learning sitting trot. You will start hanging on with your legs and thus pull your knees up. Even when you are not hanging on with them, your knees will tend to come forward because your back is not relaxed and supple enough yet to let you keep your pelvis vertical without compensating by bringing your legs forward. You may start slipping to the outside and try to compensate for this by dropping your inside shoulder. This puts your seat farther to the outside making you out of balance with the horse. You may take a death grip on the saddle, making it impossible to relax.

Do not worry about your legs coming forward until after you have the feel and can actively follow the horse's back motion. Then you can start getting

your knees lowered where they belong. However, relax your legs every time you start hanging on with them—just let them hang. Every time you start slipping to the outside, stretch your inside leg down and your inside shoulder up—stretch that whole side down and up just like stretching when you get out of bed in the morning. That will put you back in balance with the horse.

Be sure the hand you use on the saddle is always the outside one so your shoulders will stay in line with the horse's shoulders—the outside one slightly ahead of the inside one. At the same time pull the inside hip slightly forward each time it gets behind the outside one. These two things keep you straight with the horse when riding on a circle.

Rotate your head occasionally to relax your neck; rotate your shoulders and your feet, finishing each rotation by letting each of these drop relaxed into place. Breathe in rhythm with the horse's strides at a comfortable rate. Just concentrating on your breathing can help everything else fall into place. If the horse raises his head, making the trotting rough, post for a few strides to rest his back. You can easily post without stirrups without gripping with your knees, because keeping them lowered wedges them onto the horse each time you swing your hips through your elbows.

When you are relaxed and sitting the slow trot easily, you can begin to ride more actively by pushing each side of your pelvis just a little farther forward than the horse takes it. He takes it forward and you start pushing with your back on that side so that you complement his action. Relax and follow through on the other side. However, do not try to initiate the action yourself. Simply feel for the rhythm and give it a little push. Do not push so hard that you pull your knees up and get tense. Do not push from side to side—it is always a forward push. When sitting trot is done correctly, you cannot tell by looking that it is alternate seatbones—it looks like both together, but the incorrect side-to-side motion is always obvious.

It is very difficult to learn sitting trot without having a picture of it in your mind. Pictures just will not show you the action; so if you get a chance to watch a dressage show or clinic, do so. Not every sitting trot you see will be correct, but you can observe them all for the rider's suppleness in the waist, closeness of seat to saddle and relaxation. Like any athletic endeavor, the one that looks most effortless is probably the best.

When do you start sitting your horse's trot? If you feel for it, the horse himself will tell you. He will literally pull you down into the saddle. This will be when he is stepping under behind, rhythmically and relaxed, with lowered head (neck slightly above parallel), and his back swinging. This swing is a rippling up and down but is often described as side-to-side because it is alternating. It is this swing that carries one seatbone and then the other forward, and it becomes more pronounced but smoother as the horse's work progresses correctly.

When the horse invites you to sit, you can accept the invitation for only a few strides at first. He will let you know how many by stiffening his back, making it harder to sit. Immediately start posting, sitting again when invited. Gradually you can sit for more and more strides until, after he is warmed up, most of your trot work will be sitting.

There are times when we ride the trot sitting before the horse invites us down. This is usually for only a few strides to help a horse balance in going through a corner, or to drive a horse forward more effectively when he is having a reluctant streak. Often it is easier to get the canter sitting than posting, but that depends on the relaxation and suppleness of you and your horse. It does not hurt to try sitting whenever you think it can help the horse's performance.

In warming up your horse each time you ride, check out each thing you have taught him in its proper order. Start loosening him up with a walk on loose rein a couple of times around the arena, paying attention to keeping him on the track and walking forward fairly well, not just wandering around sleepily. Then take your contact and trot him forward, checking him for relaxed, rhythmic, long strides; for yielding to the bit, bending on the circle and corners; long canter strides and chewing the reins out of your hands when you come down to the walk.

Just because he did everything well in short order yesterday, do not expect to go on from there today. *If any step in the check-out gives trouble, stay with it until it is going well. More advanced work will not be any good if the basics are not good.* This check-out tells you what is needed for the day's work; but as the training progresses so the basics are firmly established, it will simply be a warm-up exercise.

Kathy Hansen and Watirah. In the warm-up stage, Watirah is tense and above the bit.

Now Watirah is relaxed and yielding to the bit and ready for the day's lesson.

After the actual control of the horse has been confirmed in your back and legs, you can loosen up your horse in walk, trot and canter on a loose rein before starting the check-out. The progression of training that takes you to this stage starts with using your back and legs properly during all riding, together with using the reins to indicate direction and balance only—never to force the horse to turn, slow down or stop. Then toward the end of each workout, you can start asking the horse to halt from the free walk on loose rein by using your back and legs only. This is a check to see if your work has been correct and the horse is understanding.

Another thing to check is how you half-halt and the response you get. Be sure your half-halts are with your back and that any hand action is merely connected to your back action. Your hands must never pull back. You should be able to feel your horse's carriage improve when you half-halt him. From these things you reach the stage of warm-up on loose rein.

By now your horse should have given up turning his head to one side, grossly dropping contact. Instead he should be stretching into the bit, seeking contact himself. If you have consistently maintained contact, yielded by softening your hands when he yields and let him chew the reins out of your hands when you're ready to rest him with the free walk, he should be seeking contact. Check this out by driving him forward when the contact drops. This should put him back up to the bit.

If your horse reliably goes up to the bit when you drive him forward, and if you're using all your aids properly in turning corners, then your horse should be starting to go on the outside rein. You can check his progress on this by moving your inside hand forward along his neck as you turn a corner. If he responds to all your aids and stretches into that outside rein so he turns the corner smoothly, then he is going on the outside rein. If you are going straight on the track and the horse continues to go straight

Carolyn Carroll and Ibn Jo Kar. This is only a test. Ibn continues on the corner with the inside contact dropped. He is going on the outside rein.

when you move your inside hand forward, then he is going on the outside rein.

This is only a test. Lots of people say, "I'm training my horse to leg cues and I don't use the reins at all." The only place this could earn you points is in cutting classes. You can't get proper collection, extension, impulsion or lateral figures such as sidepass, turn on the haunches and turn on the forehand without the reins. It's true we ride mostly with our seat and legs, but the horse must accept the bit in order for us to modify his performance.

So loose rein work can be done during warming up, several times during work to let the horse stretch out his muscles (free walk), or out on the trail as a relaxing thing. All exacting work must be done on contact.

10

IMPULSION, LATERAL MOVEMENTS, BACKING

The thing I missed most in Southern California was the winter snow and winds and ice. Before you shake your heads in disbelief, let me continue. After winter, comes spring. The snow melts, the grass greens, the breezes turn balmy and the robins sing. It is good to be alive! It made me feel like running and leaping and cavorting. In short, spring put a spring in my step. I am sure we all have days, no matter where we live or what the weather, when we feel so full of God's blessings that we spring with every step we take.

What has all this got to do with training a horse? Impulsion! We and our horses can go forward willingly and relaxed day after day through training and habit, but spring in our steps expresses a joy of living. This is what impulsion is—still going forward willingly and relaxed but springing upward with every stride.

We develop impulsion in the horse through training. Naturally, a wormy, underfed, neglected horse is not going to feel like springing upward with every stride, but impulsion is not just a feeling of the oats. That kind of expression of joy is often tense, disconcerting to the rider and a thing of the past once the edge is off. True impulsion does not come from just a mood or an overabundance of energy, but from a development of physical fitness and willing response to the rider's aids.

The system of training I have been taking you through is designed to develop the horse's fitness step-by-step. (I know you take care of the feeding, grooming, worming, etc.) It is a program for developing an equine athlete. It is also designed to develop the horse's understanding in such a way that happy obedience becomes a habit with him. So now that your horse will go forward rhythmically relaxed, yielding to the bit, accepting contact and responding to your aids, you can ask for a little impulsion by pushing him a little more onto the bit without losing any of the former way of going. Just push him gently each stride without moving your hands forward or back. Coax him to put more push into his work.

As with all new exercises, you cannot expect the horse to maintain his impulsion continuously from the moment he gets it. It must be developed gradually as his muscles develop and must be developed into an habitual way of moving. While you can get a few strides with impulsion by using strong driving aids, it is better to get it gradually, being thankful for a little spring and looking forward to more "bloom" as the horse's training and physique develop. Do not ever expect or ask for impulsion during warm-up—all athletes must loosen up their muscles before they can perform well.

The feel of impulsion is more upwardness without loss of rhythm, relaxation and forwardness. It is a softer, easier ride like a car with new shocks. It comes from behind with the horse responding to your softly driving seat by pushing himself up to your elastic contact with his mouth. The horse going with impulsion is a happy pusher.

Before the horse can start to develop impulsion, he must develop more suppleness and balance. Circles, corners and frequent changes of gaits began this training. As soon as the horse begins to do this fairly easily, it is time to add exercises to teach him to respond laterally—that is, sideways—to our aids. These exercises are turn on the forehand, leg yielding and turn on the haunches. The first two teach the horse to respond to an active outside-positioned leg and to step well under with his hind legs. They lead to the third which helps the horse balance toward the rear. All three of them aid in developing suppleness and balance. They also prepare the horse for the sidepass and halfpass. All of these things make the horse useful to you under almost any circumstances.

When riding on a circle and through corners, you have been moving your outside leg back to prevent the horse's haunches falling out. This is a passive use of your leg. When he pushed against your outside leg so you had to tap or roll your heel, your leg became active. Now we want to go a step farther and get him to move his haunches to the right when we actively use a left outside leg and vice versa. This can be started at the halt with a turn on the forehand, which means the horse moves his haunches to the side while his forefeet stay in one very small area—but not stuck to the ground.

The best time to start this is toward the end of a ride when he is relaxed and responsive. Halt him with his head straight into the side of a barn or high fence, so he will not try to step forward causing you to tense up and pull on the reins. You just sit relaxed and ask him to yield to the bit with an indirect rein on the left, maintaining contact with the right rein. This gets him to flex his head just barely to the left as well as yield. You must have both yielding and flexion but no bend in his neck. That left rein is not to be used to turn him. Now slide your left leg into the outside position and deliberately roll your heel up against his side. Do not take your right leg off your horse.

Author and Iam. Initially make use of a barrier to help the horse learn to move his haunches away from your outside leg instead of stepping forward.

Vicki Navarra and Mission Ridge. The turn on the forehand out in the open, done here in the walk to overcome the horse's tendency to cross behind his other leg instead of in front of it.

As he steps to the right with his left hind leg, relax all aids and pet him. Move him off in the walk, bring him back into the original position and ask him to do it again. Again pet him and move him off; and when you return this time, reverse your aids and ask him to move his haunches to the left. After two successes in this direction with walking in between, move him off in a good free walk and reward him by stopping work for the day.

If your horse does not respond to your aids, reinforce your heel by touching him with the whip on the same side. Do not try to turn his head more to get him to step over. *It is very important that you flex his neck only at the poll, that you stay relaxed and that he understands he must respond to your active leg. It is very important that you keep your other leg on him, not only to limit his movement to one step at a time but so you can use it to drive him forward when doing leg yielding.* If you use the whip at the same time you roll your heel up, he will get the connection. Eventually you will not need the whip aid, but you will find that for some time he will not respond to your left leg when the whip is in your right hand and vice versa. Having the whip on the "wrong" side confuses him early in the game.

As soon as your horse will make this turn on the forehand at a barrier, it is best to go on to leg yielding. Gradually it will develop so you can make the turn halted anywhere, but for now we want to keep the horse moving. In leg yielding to the right, the whole horse is flexed slightly to the left and positioned at a twenty to thirty degree angle to the left of his direction of travel. Both his front and hind left legs will cross over in front of their respective right ones. (In shoulder-in the whole horse is flexed more and his hind legs travel straight ahead while his front legs cross over.)

There are three situations where you can easily ask for leg yielding. You can turn from the short side of the arena about ten feet before you reach the corner. As you come parallel to the track, ask for the leg yield, moving sideways over to the track as

Kathy Hansen and Watirah.
Leg yielding to the left down the track.

you are moving forward. Or you can turn the regular corner, staying in the bend until you are turned in about twenty to thirty degrees from the track and continue down the track in leg yield. A third option is to go on a circle and ask the horse to move his haunches out as his forelegs travel on the track of the circle, his hind legs making a larger circle.

There is one way to ask for leg yielding to the right: your left leg moves back to the outside position, your right leg moves into the regular position and your left rein is indirect. As the horse's body swings to the right, your left heel rolls up to move his haunches to the right. As his body swings to the left, your right leg drives him forward. If necessary, the whip can reinforce your left leg as

Author and Iam. From a turn short of the corner, leg yielding to the right to the track. My right leg should be on the horse.

From a short turn leg yielding to the left.

your heel rolls up. Early on, an occasional right leading rein can help the horse move forward. All systems are reversed for leg yielding to the left.

While I stated that the horse's inside legs cross over in front of the outside legs, it is more important for the horse to continue going forward with rhythm and to step well under himself with his inside hind leg, than to step far sideways. At first he may step only in front of his outside feet, but this little beginning is great if he is not allowed to lose his forwardness and rhythm. It is better to get a couple of strides of leg yield and then move the horse straight forward than to keep trying for more at the expense of forwardness and rhythm. More yielding strides will come with practice.

Start in the walk, getting into the swing of the horse's rhythm and then go into leg yielding so that your aids stay rhythmic. When the horse understands in the walk, go on to the trot since leg yielding is easier to do at that gait after you both understand it. I found it easier initially to post the trot, rising as the horse's inside shoulder goes forward. This automatically makes the lateral aid properly timed—when that hind leg is coming forward and so can move sideways—even though the driving aid will be simultaneous. When the horse is ready for sitting trot, your aids will alternate as in the walk. It is helpful to have a friend tell you what results you are getting so you can develop a feel for the horse's leg stepping under.

Turn on the forehand can be done halted and in the walk. Leg yielding can be done in the walk, trot and canter. Turn on the haunches can be done halted, walking and cantering, but not in the trot since the poor horse would then tie his legs in knots.

In dressage terminology the turn on the haunches

105

Author and Pi Dough. A very poor turn on the haunches. I let the horse lose his balance
and tried to pull him through the turn.

in the walk and the canter are called walking and canter pirouettes respectively, and must be done without interruption of the walk or canter footfall sequences. If this exercise is to evolve into the rollback, then these criteria should be followed; but taking it on to the stockhorse pivot, it is only important that the horse pivot around his inside hind leg in the final training. Any horse can be trained to do both if he is taught the pirouettes first as he should be.

Whether you are a dressage purist or simply want a usin' horse, the turn on the haunches is best started in the walk against the side of a building or high fence. Brush or trees will do for a barrier just so long as the horse cannot get his head over or under them. Using such a barrier as an aid to understanding can prevent a lot of unwanted neck bending and helps the horse shift his balance toward the rear so

you do not develop the tendency to pull him back with the reins. Neck bending and rein pulling are gross errors.

In this exercise you eventually want the horse to turn with his hind feet staying in one small area. Obviously you do not want his haunches moving out to the right as you turn him to the left, because then he would just turn like a merry-go-round horse spinning on his pole. So you have to move your outside leg into the outside position to hold those haunches in line. This will help bend the horse around your inside leg so his whole spine is bent slightly in the direction of the turn. You only have two legs—one on each side of the horse—so you can see that you cannot help him through the turn by kicking him in the shoulder at the same time you hold his haunches in. This shoulder kicking is a false aid that seems to work at times but leaves ev-

106

A very good walking turn on the haunches. Everybody in balance and the horse properly bent.

erything up to the horse's own devices. Do not get in the habit.

Walk your horse parallel to the wall about six to eight feet out from it. As you start into the turn toward the wall, move your outside leg into position, drive strongly and rhythmically and turn the horse with a leading rein at the same time you bring your outside rein barely against his neck. If you look right back where you want to go, your hand should cross the right amount. Do not lose your contact and do not try to pull him through the turn. Simply keep him moving through rhythmic driving. As he starts coming around to 180 degrees, relax the aids as you keep driving.

At first the horse will make about a 4-foot circle with his hind feet. Do not worry about that. Do not worry if he seems a little slow to turn at first; just keep driving and the wall will help him make it.

The main thing is to avoid pulling him around with the inside rein. The leading rein helps him, but it is the combination of the outside rein brought closer to his neck, the outside leg holding his haunches and the driving him forward onto the bit that gets the results. You will know it is a good turn on the haunches if it feels as if that merry-go-round pole is now just back of your seat and he brought his whole body around it all in one piece.

You can dispense with the wall, making the turns out in the open as soon as the horse understands your aids. Gradually you can dispense with the leading rein, just keeping your hands in front of you and turning your upper body in the direction of the turn. This will automatically put your hands in the proper position. Gradually the horse will be able to make shorter turns so his hind feet stay in a smaller area. Be sure you keep him moving rhythmically "for-

When the horse's head is up and his back down like this, it is impossible for him to back easily or properly.

ward." *Be careful at all times to avoid bending his neck. It is better to drop inside contact altogether and finish the turn on the outside rein only, than to pull on the inside rein.* You can turn him from the halt after he is well-schooled in walking pirouettes.

We have not yet asked the horse to back. It is best not to teach him this before he thoroughly understands the aids for turn on the haunches because then you often get steps toward the rear in the turn. While the horse must shift his balance toward the rear for a turn on the haunches, you get it by driving him onto the bit even in the halt. Simply close your legs firmly on him without yielding your hands forward but with closing your fingers. You can feel the horse "move" toward the rear as he squats and engages his hocks, but he must not take a step

back. Now he is balanced and ready to turn.

But to get back to backing. There is no big deal to it when the horse is this far along. *The horse must be halted at attention, relaxed and yielding to the bit.* When you have him like this, simply squeeze your hands shut, elbows at your sides; and staying quite relaxed, close your legs firmly on his sides. As he starts making the step back, relax the aids. If you want another step back, start the aids again as his feet start to go to the ground. He should step back with definite stride with diagonal pairs just as in trotting, but without the suspension between the strides.

While a horse should spring forward, he should never fall back. He should step back willingly and freely, neither dragging his feet nor rushing back.

108

First get the horse to yield and then ask him to back by aiding with your legs. This horse would step back more freely with the rider more relaxed and using more leg aid. Otherwise it is well done.

Val Parnell and Pepper. Pepper has yielded and stepped back freely.

At first ask for only one stride back. Gradually get two and then three. Avoid backing him a great deal. Train him in backing after he is relaxed and working well in a lesson. He will not step back for you if you are tense or if he is tense, inattentive or not yielding to the bit. Make sure all systems are go before asking him to go backward.

When a horse is well-trained to back this way, you can sit quietly on him, aiding him forward and at the same time tell him whether it is really forward or back you want simply by relaxing or fixing your hands. This is how it was done in the "good ole days" by the vaqueros, not running the horse backward with obvious jerks on the reins. No one should see your aids. They swear you do it with ESP; but then that is the ultimate in all riding—just sitting there a part of your horse, seemingly just thinking your commands and getting instant, relaxed obedience. With instant play, who needs replay!

11

STRAIGHTNESS, EXTENSION, COLLECTION

Coming down the home stretch to the finish, we will now get straightness, extension and collection. These things complete the horse's basic training, making him ready for any specialized training. Do not think that your horse should get this far along in his training—zip, zip, zip—just like that. Progress must be according to the ability and understanding of the rider and the horse, not according to any time schedule.

Basic straightness means that a horse steps forward with his hind feet on exactly the same lines as their respective front feet, keeping his spine in line with the track he is traveling whether it is straight or curved. In the final analysis straightness means he will go where we point him in the manner we ask without wandering off the straight and narrow or evading with any part of his body, neck or head.

Now the horse is not a piece of machinery that we can adjust with micrometers, feeler gauges and

Peggy Barcaglia and Rafe. Trying to collect a horse or slow him down with the reins alone restricts the movement of his hind legs.

variable metric wrenches to make him go precisely true. He is mind, muscle and emotions. Therefore we spend this time and effort to gradually train him to accept all the aids obediently so we can use them in whatever combination is needed at any moment to get the best performance from the horse. When he accepts all the aids, we say he is "between our hands and legs" or he is "on the aids." It means he will step straight up to the bit equally on both sides.

Since the horse is not a push-button robot—nor do we want him to be—he will never perform with absolute perfection; but when he is on the aids, we can tell him to straighten up and fly right when he has his days and little ways. For instance, if he kinks

his body out to the right saying he would rather veer off to the left, all you have to do is close your right leg on him more to make him step up to the bit and go straight. And that is the answer to all his deviousness—push him up to the bit. Do not try to straighten him by pulling the bit back to him.

A horse that is going straight in whatever he is doing feels as if all parts of him are working in unison. He is "all in one piece." Whether he is going on a straight track, turning corners or doing more difficult things such as running barrels, he must do it as all one horse, not two or three horses going in all different directions. The straight horse is the culmination of correct training. We therefore

At the same point in trot stride and pushed up to the bit, the horse strides under behind and carries himself with balance. More acceptance of the aids plus greater physical development lead to proper collection.

don't try to twist and hammer him into being straight, but get him to accept the aids more and more so he'll be straight, or can be reminded to go straight, because he does accept them.

That is why we just now speak of getting straightness. We've been working on it all this time in all the training we've been doing. We finally get it all together when the horse reliably accepts this training.

Extension and collection are usually misunderstood. In both of these the horse's rhythm should stay the same as his rhythm in the regular gaits, although it can be just slightly slower in the extended gaits. "But," you say, "what I want is to go faster or slower!" The best way for you to understand what I'm saying is to walk alongside another person. Both of you start out in a regular walk, counting the rhythm. Then one of you lengthen his stride while still maintaining the same rhythm. That's true extension. Who went the fastest? Now do it again, and this time one of you shorten his stride while maintaining the same rhythm. That's true collection. Who went the slowest?

Let me stress right here that very few of us will ever ask for or get true extension and collection in the Grand-Prix-Dressage sense of the terms. We will probably get only lengthening and balance by dressage definition. But most of us do not need Grand Prix Dressage Horses, so I will use the terms extension and collection to mean the high level of performance we want from our usin' horses. Ignore the screams of the purists unless you have Grand Prix ambitions.

The trouble is that even when a person gets a chance to see correct collection, he thinks only about how slowly the horse is going and how pretty it arches its neck. So the rider goes home, sets the horse's head and pulls on the reins again and again to train his horse to go poking along. Then he is real proud of his collected horse, not aware that pulling on the reins has restricted the horse's stride behind and has discouraged the horse from moving forward

113

onto the bit. The least closing of the fingers on the reins will cause this horse to stick his hind feet in the ground and slow down. The only way he will go forward more is to give him rein.

Another bad result of pulling on the reins instead of riding the horse forward onto the bit, whether it is for collection or just simple riding, is that it enhances or even causes a ewe neck. This is because it develops the muscles on the underside of the horse's neck instead of those on top of his neck. All of this work I have been telling you about develops the proper muscles all over the horse so he will carry himself more easily and more beautifully under saddle and even when he is running loose.

My ex-horse, Dos Reales, is a very good example. He is built with a high head, low back and hind legs working out behind him. When I was working him regularly, he would run around playing with his head lower, his neck correctly arched, his back raised and his hind legs stepping under. Now that I have not ridden him for well over a year, he is back to his original way of going. His original muscular development has taken over again.

In correct collection the horse takes shorter strides in the same rhythm as his regular gait with at least the same amount of energy, therefore he lifts himself higher. In order to do all this he must balance more toward the rear and bend all the joints in his hindquarters so that his haunches are lowered. This raises the whole forehand producing that pretty, arched-neck picture.

There are horses that are naturally excitable that have been allowed—or encouraged—to stay that way. These horses, collected with the reins, give the appearance of correct collection. But their rhythm is quick and tense, and they're unyielded to the bit, charging ahead at any relaxing on the reins. When a horse is relaxed and yielded to the bit, the better balanced he becomes, the lighter he gets on the reins because he's in a better position to carry himself and make changes in gaits, speed and direction.

We've been working on balance with exercises and pushing him onto the bit. This work leads to collection eventually, but he must be balanced for extension, too. He shouldn't extend by falling forward because you would have to help hold him up with the bit and he would have to speed up his rhythm to try to keep from falling forward. While we continually work on balance, we start the horse on extension before asking him for collection because lengthening is easier for him to do physically. Also, we want to maintain his will to go forward because collection is dependent upon this—not upon pulling on the reins to slow him down.

The feel of a correct extension is the same feel you get watching a motorboat smoothly pick up speed. The stern sinks and the bow rises and everything smooths out as the speed increases. In the horse the rhythm remains the same or gets slightly slower and he lengthens his whole body as he lengthens his stride.

You may have noticed by now that when you want a horse to move a certain way, you do it yourself, so to speak. For example, if you want a turn on the haunches, you move yourself over with the same sinking in your haunches that you will feel in your horse's haunches, and you get a good turn. I hesitate to say this at the beginning of a new maneuver because riders then tend to tense up and overdo it. But as you get the feel of any movement, you tend to do it yourself automatically.

So when I ask a pupil to ask for extension, I say "go like a motorboat!" You should think of the feel and sink into the saddle as you firmly and smoothly push each stride farther forward and lower your hands. The horse sinks his haunches and lengthens his stride.

The horse must be well into the day's lesson so he feels tuned and ready. You cannot force him to lengthen—he must feel balanced and willing to move freely forward. Then you ask for about three strides of lengthening, either on a long side or across

114

Kathy Hansen and Watirah. This is Watirah's regular trot.

Watirah in lengthened trot—the beginning stage of developing extension.

Carolyn Carroll and Ibn Jo Kar. Ibn Jo Kar in the regular trot—called the working trot in dressage terms.

Betty Bevan and Shemali. Shemali is similar in conformation to Ibn Jo Kar. Compare her extended trot with Ibn's regular trot.

the diagonal in a change of hand. There is neither time nor incentive for lengthening on a short side. The transition from regular trot to extension must flow, so you must flow into the aids. Sink down and firmly p-u-s-h, p-u-s-h, p-u-s-h. Then float back to normal so the horse floats back to the regular trot strides.

Two or three times in each direction of three good lengthened strides is enough work at a time. Gradually you can get better lengthening plus more strides of it, but it is work for the horse. It taxes the horse's muscles and it cannot be done overnight without discomfort to him. Develop more lengthening and increase the number of strides gradually.

Trotting over cavalletti, gradually widening the spacing, can help get extension. You will not want to do it exclusively this way, but it can help. Remember to ask for the lengthening as you are going into the first cavalletto and to avoid the poles when you are asking for regular trot.

The canter strides are lengthened much the same way. At the point of pushing forward with your back, you push a little farther as you lower your hands. In both the trot and the canter allow the horse to stretch his head and neck slightly since the whole framework of the horse should lengthen. However, throwing away the contact would simply cause him to rush with quicker steps. Firm up your hands some if he rushes. On the other hand, if he leans on the bit, you need to push more without yielding more with your hands.

When the horse is responding well to extensions, you can begin collection. In order to collect well a horse must go forward willingly and accept the bit willingly. This is a more difficult exercise for him because it takes more physical effort. In order to collect and still keep the same rhythm, the horse not only must shorten his stride but he must push upward more. That is work!

To get collection in the trot you push more each

stride. In the canter you push more each time your seat goes forward. This push is with a lifting sort of feeling as if you expect the horse to lift you higher. At the same time you elastically keep his face in the vertical, and he should get lighter on the bit as he collects. If he leans on the bit, he needs more pushing. If he bores into the bit, he is not accepting contact properly and needs more work leading up to collection: that is, shifting his balance toward the rear.

I have already given you some exercises that improve the horse's balance. These are transitions in gaits, leg yielding, turn on the haunches, cavalletti work and the use of half-halts. Besides continuing these exercises, you can gradually make the circles smaller in all gaits, make frequent changes of direction and frequent changes of exercises. These all help because the horse himself will try to maintain his balance to be ready for them. Aid early and smoothly so you do not startle him with last-minute changes.

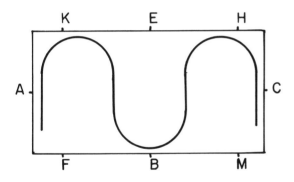

There are more exercises that help in suppling the horse and improving his balance. The serpentine of three loops across the width of the arena can be done soon after you are doing the change out of the circle and the flat serpentine. The more loops you put in these serpentines across the arena the more difficult the exercise, so build up to more loops gradually. Be sure to bend to the arc on each end

and go straight across toward the opposite side, starting your arc at each end in time to make it smooth and even.

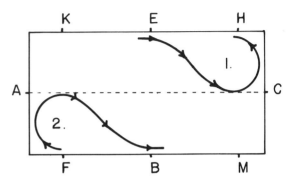

The reverse half circle (1) and the half circle (2) can be done in that order. The reverse half circle gives your horse a visual aid to help him bend and balance better and can lead into walking pirouettes turning into the side of the arena. In the half circle the horse must bend through obedience to your aids, so it is more difficult for both of you. It leads into walking pirouettes turning away from the side of the arena.

Although the horse can walk through a change through the circle quite early in training, trotting through it is far more difficult because of the short turns. You will find that in order to do this on a 60-foot circle you will have to ride sitting and drive him onto the bit to get him balanced enough. Be sure to come far enough around in the first bend to be able to make the figure symmetrical. The horse should take one straight stride in the middle. The only way you can get this is to reverse your aids for the opposite bend as you approach the middle, so he takes that straight stride in the process of reversing his bend.

In any canter work involving change of hand such as figure eights and serpentines, come to the trot in the middle for two or three strides to ask for the change of lead. As the horse balances better, ask

117

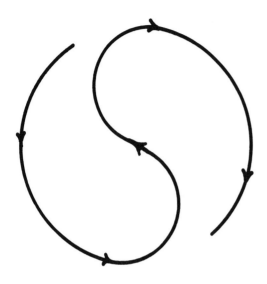

strides on the short side. The short side is a mental stimulus for collection just as the long side or the diagonal is a mental stimulus for extension. Be satisfied with just a little shortening of stride in the same rhythm. All improvement must be gradual. Get extensions and collections in the trot first, the canter next and finally in the walk. The walk is the hardest gait to work in since it lacks momentum no matter how good it is. The walk, like the other gaits, must not ever be rushed but must be rhythmic, relaxed and forward.

As the horse can extend and collect better, you can work him in transitions of regular, extended, regular and collected gaits. These transitions also help his balance when you flow into them so there is no jerk in shifting gears.

So far the work I have outlined should take about two years to complete, starting with a green 4-year old, but it can be useful in many instances before it is completed. It is also helpful to know how these things apply in special fields so you do not get impatient to try the specialties before the horse is ready. Just like our lives, all horse training should be built upon a solid rock foundation.

for the change of lead through a walk. Also, ask for the canter from the walk on first one lead and then the other, going straight. These prepare him for flying changes later on when he is really collected. Canter pirouettes must also wait for collection.

When you ask for collection, ask for about three

Part Four
Specializations

FINISHING FOR PLEASURE/TRAIL HORSE

Except to those few misguided souls who get their kicks from jerking about on a wild-eyed horse that is a menace to every denizen of horsedom, the horse that is easily controllable at all times in all situations is really a pleasure to ride. The aim of all this training I have been telling you about is just such a pleasure horse, one that is your partner, happily using his energy to work with you, responding as if the two of you are of one mind. Any finishing touches and any more advanced training from here on are according to your personal desires and ambitions.

Whether you simply want your horse for your own pleasure and trail riding, or have more specialized goals such as competing at barrels, endurance rides, stock horse, jumping or dressage, the sound foundation is this basic training. From here on I want to go into the finishing touches for the pleasure-trail horse, the relation and application of this training to specializations and even how to ride

Vicki Navarra and Mission Ridge. Mission then—

And now, after two years of this basic dressage training which develops the whole horse.

a dressage test for those of you who have become interested.

The main finishing touch is neckreining, which is a handy thing for all horses, English as well as western, to know. When you neckrein properly and ride dressage style properly, you can ride the same horse either way you choose. When the horse accepts the outside rein and your leg aids, he is well on his way to neckreining. My colt accepts the outside rein most of the time now and already neckreins in the walk without any formal training in the subject.

Neckreining has nothing to do with pressure of the rein on the horse's neck. It is true that a neckreining horse will turn on a loose rein at the touch of the outside rein on his neck—plus whatever other turning aids you have taught him—but the real reason the horse turns is because he has accepted the outside rein. (Remember the test of riding through the corner with a dropped inside rein?) So in neckreining correctly you never use pressure on the horse's neck, and the only time you ever neckrein up in the middle of his neck is when you must carry something in your reining hand, such as the coils of a lead rope or lass rope.

A horse turns because he accepts ALL the turning aids: outside rein, inside driving leg, outside leg holding the haunches in. I often hear people say, "I'm teaching my horse to respond to leg aids." This is great! A horse must respond to leg aids to be really under control, but the trouble is that these people usually mean leg aids without rein aids.

A horse turns well—or does any maneuver well—because he is balanced toward the rear. In explaining collection, I showed that it requires more energy, not less. So with more energy coming from the rear, the bit must be there to accept that energy and direct it into the amount of balance (collection) needed for each movement you ask the horse to perform. *Always remember that it is the horse's acceptance of all the aids that makes him a real pleasure to ride.*

If you do not use pressure on the horse's neck and do not neckrein up in the middle of his neck, how do you neckrein? Actually it is quite simple. On the finished horse you keep your reining hand in front of you just barely above and behind the saddle horn or pommel. Make every turn similar to a turn on the haunches—push the horse onto the bit to balance him toward the rear; drive with your inside leg; put your outside leg back and look in the direction of the turn, letting your upper body turn according to the size of the corner.

All of this automatically puts your reining hand in the proper position—barely across the horse's withers—to neckrein him through the turn. No pressure on the horse's neck is needed. If the horse doesn't turn well, it's because he wasn't balanced enough or bent enough in his spine or going forward good enough. Pressure on his neck will never make him turn better.

The only way that neckreining differs from two-fisted riding is that you let your outside hand cross the horse's withers slightly—an instance of using the indirect rein on the outside. You start teaching a horse to neckrein after he has accepted the outside rein and while you're still holding the reins one in each hand. Along with letting your outside hand cross slightly over the withers, use all the turning aids I have repeatedly described. Whenever the horse needs help in making a turn, use your inside leading rein briefly. Don't bridge your reins the way present day western riders do because this would hamper your using the leading rein.

When the horse no longer needs help with the leading rein, you can cross the reins in one hand, letting the other rein come in under your thumb and out under your little finger. Then you can help him turn when needed by a little twist of the wrist to barely tighten the inside rein. When he no longer needs help neckreining, you can hold both reins together coming in under your little finger and out under your thumb. Never hold them coming in on

A common error when riding one-handed is to twist the hips and shoulders, causing the horse to go crooked.

Peggy Barcaglia and Rafe. Help the horse learn to neckrein by using a leading rein, not by applying pressure on his neck.

top of your hand because this will cause the horse to raise his nose (go above the bit). Also avoid sitting twisted in the saddle and twisted in your shoulders when riding one-handed.

A curb bit is not any real use on a pleasure or trail horse; but, unfortunately, horse show rules call for the curb in such classes. Hopefully they'll wise up someday and make the snaffle optional, but for now you've got to bridle your horse to show him. If you do not plan to show, forget it. If you have trained yourself and your horse correctly in the basics, he will work well all his life in the snaffle. If you do bridle him so you can show him, continue to do most of your work in the snaffle to keep him sweet, working him in the curb just enough to assure good, understanding performance in it.

Never put a horse in the curb bit for the purpose of getting better control. Only proper training can give you reliable control, not forcing the horse into obedience through pain. The curb is for refinement only—and because archaic show rules require it. Never put the horse in the curb before he is fully trained in the basics. Never try to teach the horse a new thing or correct a fault with the curb. Do it first in the snaffle.

The proper way to put the English horse in the curb is with the full bridle: curb bit and snaffle separate in the same bridle. Pelham bits—those with slots or rings for curb and snaffle reins but only one mouthpiece, which includes the so-called "western snaffle"—are very poor bits because the horse cannot tell the difference between the curb and the snaffle to respond accordingly, and because you cannot bend the horse laterally with the bar mouthpiece. The broken mouthpiece of the "western snaffle" is a nutcracker on the horse's bars when used as a curb—very painful!

You can buy a full bridle or put one together by using your snaffle bridle and adding the curb bridle and a cavesson. Remove the dropped noseband because it is never used with the curb. Do not use a thin snaffle because it discourages the horse from staying on the bit. There is plenty of room in the horse's mouth for the thick snaffle and the curb. All this applies to western riders too, if your curb bit has thin cheeks between the mouthpiece and the headstall ring to accommodate the snaffle.

The curb bit should be made of steel with a thick, straight bar mouthpiece. If it has a port, that port should be low and broad and the sides of the mouthpiece should still be at right angles to the cheeks. The best leverage ratio is 3:2, certainly no more than 2:1, measured from the rein rings to the center of the mouthpiece and from there to the attachment of the curb strap or chain. Any greater leverage than this is too severe for any horse.

You can use a curb strap or a curb chain. The strap should be three-eighths to one-half inch wide; the curb chain should be the double link type. Be sure to twist it flat so there are no lumps or bumps to pinch and poke the horse's chin groove. Adjust the strap or chain so there is a forty-five degree angle between the positions of the shanks when hanging completely loose and when taken up completely snug. The snaffle mouthpiece goes on top of the curb mouthpiece and the curb strap or chain goes below the snaffle.

You should not have any problems holding the four reins. You already have the snaffle reins in place between your ring fingers and your little fingers. Now pick up the curb reins under your little fingers, letting them come through your fists and out under your thumbs. Western riders, your horse should be fully trained to neckrein before starting him in the curb, so you can hold both snaffle reins together in one hand as mentioned and add the curb reins together under your little finger.

Give the horse a chance to get used to the curb by starting with light contact, giving him just the feel of the curb while controlling him with the snaffle. Start him with beginning exercises and gradually take him up through more advanced ones. If he is to go in the curb alone, start letting the snaffle reins looser when he is doing all his work on contact on both sets of reins. Keep the snaffle on him until you no longer need it to help him out, but still work him on the snaffle alone during all this training and the rest of his life. It will keep his performances top notch.

You now have a pleasure show horse, both English and western. Decked out in your western finery, you give your horse a slightly longer rein to let him stretch out for the flatter western gaits. Because your horse moves forward with relaxed energy, accepting the bit with light contact, he shows he is a pleasure to ride. He swings his back and you sit his trot so easily, yet he is striding under without rushing away, showing he is not wearying you with psuedo slow gaits that drag along. His lope is long and easy, no longer four ticky-tacky beats that make him look stifled.

And those leads! No longer do you have to turn your horse's head to the rail, lean over and give a mighty shove, then check to make sure you got it. You have progressed from getting the lead on the circle to getting it in the corner and now can get it going straight simply by bending your horse slightly around your inside leg, half-halt and canter. Whatever the judge asks you to do, your horse does as if he reads your mind because he is on the aids and willing. A picture of real pleasure!

In the show ring again with English clothes and tack, you push your horse onto the bit for more collection raising his whole forehand and his action for more animation. You go through the whole thing again, posting the trot effortlessly because you are in balance with the horse, making it unnecessary for you to pull yourself high off the saddle with the reins. Now an animated picture of real pleasure!

You can win in both types of classes on the same horse if the basic training is correct. I have heard people say, "I ride my horse western with the stock saddle and English with the English saddle so he will know the difference." All they are trying to do is teach the horse two different styles of performance. With basic dressage training you can ask the horse to perform any way you want at any time under any circumstances. The possibilities are unlimited.

Whether you show your horse or just use him for your own pleasure riding, one of the main things you want to develop is mutual trust. You have been developing his trust in you by riding him without jerking him around and by developing his training according to his physical and mental progress. When riding him out on trails, you develop his trust in you by starting him on easy terrain and gradually taking him over progressively more difficult country as his ability to carry you and his confidence increase. When a situation is quite scary to your colt, do not try to whip him through it; this will only convince him he has a right to be scared. Take the time to let him look it over, leading him if necessary, and then riding him through. When a horse knows you will not get him in a bind, he will trust your judgment and go forward for you.

When you know he will go forward reliably, you will trust his judgment and avoid mistakes such as the one my aunt in Saskatchewan made. She wanted to take a shortcut across a slough. The horse said no and she emphatically said yes. The first step into the water the horse sank to his elbows, quivered there a moment and then lifted himself out and around. Like Doctor Foster, my aunt never went there again. She also learned to put more trust in her horse's judgment.

It is not blind obedience you want, just reliable obedience and mutual trust and respect. While you want your horse to have lots of experience in all kinds of terrain so that you do not have to tell him each step to take, some chores you definitely want him to do through obedience. If he does them through routine, any variation in the situation will give both of you fits.

Several years ago I had a fellow working for me who started colts on gate-opening on their first or second ride. In no time at all he had this one colt, Sitkin, lining right up beside the gate so he could open it and even manage to get it closed after going through. A short time later I was riding Sitkin and

Sitting behind the horse's center of balance, neckreining in the middle of his neck with loose rein, leaning forward—any one of these can cause loss of control.

This rider is using her seat and legs and contact to hold the horse straight while it checks out the bridge.

Author and Iam. When a horse shies at an object, trying to hold his head toward it only increases his fear and permits him to swing his body out in the path of possible danger.

With control of his body you can turn his head slightly away from the booger, keep him straight with an outside leg next to it and ride the horse straight on by.

needed to go through that gate. As I neared it, he suddenly rushed forward and lined himself up with the gate on his right. Since it was a left-handed gate, I tried everything to get him to turn around. I even rode him along the fence with it on his left; but the moment he came to the gate, he flipped himself right around.

What use is such a horse? He wasn't under my control. He was merely programmed for opening that gate in the one specific way. A similar situation was the time I was at a friend's house and she asked me to take her horse and drag a bale of hay out to the pasture horses. She had a bale hook with a rope tied to it and the hay was in the end of an old dairy barn, so all I had to do was ride up to the dock, hook a bale, take my dallies and ride off to pasture dragging the bale. Simple!

But the closest bale was a little far back from the edge and no matter what I tried, that mare would not do anything but stand headed straight into the dock. No turn on the forehand. No riding her parallel. She'd been put straight up to the dock time after time, her rider leaning far past her head to hook a bale. No way would she change that routine and she hadn't the slightest understanding of leg aids. I finally had to get off, hook the bale and get back on the horse to drag it off. If I'd had my own mare, I could have easily put either side of her parallel to the dock with a turn on the forehand, reached the bale from the saddle and been in business. Instead I'd had to dismount. How degrading!

If you have control of the horse's body, you have control of the horse; but if his head is the only thing

128

you control, you have no control at all. Control means safety, which is important—especially with the creeping crud of civilization that makes it necessary at times to use public roads for bridle trails. Suppose you're riding along a road with a car coming up behind you and a scary—to the horse—object to the right of you. The horse instinctively wants to wheel to the left to escape. If you only have control of his head, you'll instinctively turn him to the right. The horse will swing his haunches out into the path of the oncoming car and all three of you are in trouble, maybe serious trouble.

With control of the whole horse this situation is easily handled. The horse wants to turn his head away, so flex it away. This partly relieves his mind—he feels he is escaping danger. At the same time, put your right leg in the outside position to hold his haunches in line. With the horse that goes obediently forward and obeys your legs laterally, you will ride straight past the scary thing and the car will get safely by. All such shying should be handled this way whether there is danger or not.

While this is possibly an extreme case, still it should serve to show you that a horse's haunches can cause you all kinds of trouble if you cannot control them. With control of the whole horse, you can easily put him where you want him at any time—and that is real safe pleasure.

13

TRAIL CLASS GYMKHANA, ENDURANCE RIDING

I remember one time I was riding my colt, Shadow, on a cow trail around the side of a hill. The hill kept getting steeper and steeper and I should have had better sense than to go on, but I hate to backtrack. Across the little canyon ahead I could see the hill start to flatten out again. Rounding the hill to the switchback, we found that not only was it pretty well washed out but also that it had a 2-foot-thick log catty-cornered in the middle. The trail back was too narrow, steep and far to back out, even on a trained horse, let alone on this colt; but then I could ride a trained horse across or even pivot him 180 degrees over empty space to turn around. Shadow wasn't even used to carrying my weight yet!

The only thing to do was dismount, but how? That first step down on the left was the one the joke tells you to look out for. On the right was a loose dirt bank that could let me slip under the colt, which might scare him—otherwise I wasn't worried

Author and Iam. The horse should be under the rider's complete control no matter what the situation, not just programmed for each trail class obstacle.

about an Indian dismount because I always crawl all over my colts during their first saddling lessons. Talking conversationally all the time to Shadow, I wiggled around some to show him I was coming offside, put my arms around his neck as I slipped my feet out of the stirrups, and let myself rotate to come in for a landing right under his nose. No trouble—good colt!

The rest was fairly easy. I secured his reins to the saddle just so he wouldn't step in them (but long enough to give him plenty of head room), slipped my reata around his neck and picked my way across the washout. I kept my eye on Shadow to make sure he didn't try to follow too soon because colts hate to be left alone out in nowhere. When I came to the end of my rope, I persuaded him to come on over.

He was a sensible colt—picked his way across without even trying to jump—and me and my Shadow went on down the trail to find a place where I could mount.

Leading across obstacles is one of the things I always teach my horses, though not always as a case of necessity the first time. I eventually drag things, carry things, lead other horses and even swing a lass rope, although the only way I can rope a calf is to tie him up first. I don't start teaching the horse these things until I have him under reliable control. I never start a horse on a gate until he'll turn on the forehand; then I ride straight up to the gate and line him up with a turn on the forehand—sometimes on one side and sometimes on the other. If he gets nervous when I reach for the latch, I just get him

132

used to that. When he lets me open the gate, I simply push it open, ride through and dismount to close it. Later on when he'll leg yield and sidepass, I'll close the gate. *Never fight with a horse to try to teach him things.*

Everything I teach a horse is for my convenience and the most convenient thing is to have him on the aids so no strange situation starts a fight or becomes dangerous. After all, you can't foresee every situation you might get into, especially if you're like me and have an insatiable urge to explore every new trail you come to. Nor can you anticipate every cockeyed obstacle you'll run into in a trail class, so you can get your horse routined to all of them at home. Train your horse first to be on the aids, then obstacles are no obstacle.

Years ago I attended an Arabian Club trail ride and schooling show at Kellogg's in Southern California. I was riding my half-Arab mare who was trained as far as I have taken you in this series. For the trail "class" they asked us to ride across the teeter-totter used for that trick horse act. I just rode my mare straight up to the end and asked her to halt square. When I felt her relax—which is a horse's way of saying, "Thy will be done"—I asked her to step straight forward. At the tipping point I asked for the halt followed by one step forward. The teeter-totter slowly tipped and it was downhill all the rest of the way.

Later on I was living in Nevada with this same mare. In back of my place was a main irrigation canal too steep and deep to be crossed. This meant I had to ride a half mile west to a bridge on a county road to get out into the wide open spaces to ride, then run the course backward to get home. One day I happened to come back from the east along the canal and came on a cement foot bridge across it. The bridge was maybe three feet wide with 3-foot high railings. I rode Princess up to the end of it and asked her to halt and look it over. When she relaxed, we went up the two cement steps, across the bridge, down one small step and were home

free. It was much closer to home and I used it often after that.

These are examples of how this training coupled with mutual trust can take you anywhere you want to go horseback without fuss or muss. I do not remember whether anyone else made it across that teeter-totter or not, but I do know they all made lots of tracks all around the end of it trying to get their horses' heads pointed in the right direction. When you only have control of the head, the horse can sit on his haunches and whirl away or run out with his shoulder no matter where you point his head. But when you can close your legs on your horse and he will step straight up to the bit, you can tell him exactly where you want him to go and know he will go there.

Do give your horse a chance to see what he is getting into. It only takes a brief moment to relax the well-trained, trusting horse and any trail class judge worth his salt will give you more points for this approach than mechanically walking through even with the horse's head down. Lean over to go down with him if he wants to smell or feel, keeping your legs firmly on him; but then expect him to raise his head to go across while you assess the next obstacle, not looking down at the one you're crossing. Princess and I won consistently in trail classes and she never had to put her head down to inspect an obstacle. That's just present day style based on false information about a horse's vision. I never showed according to style; I always showed according to horsemanship—and won!

Don't go in trail classes, or any riding classes except dressage, with a colt to give him experience; it could be hazardous to his healthy training. For one thing, he has to be in the curb bit and he shouldn't be made to wear such a bit until he's fully trained in basics. For another, if you put him in a scary situation and can't control him properly, you have let him feel that he can't trust you to take care of him and have let him know he can get his own way. Both of these are setbacks in training.

Vicki Navarra and Mission Ridge. This basic training coupled with mutual trust can take you anywhere you want to go without fuss or muss.

Be patient. Train him first in the basics. Then it's okay to give your horse experience on show-type obstacles, but be sure he goes through because of his obedience to your aids and that you use the aids you've taught him. For instance, don't try to get him alongside the gate by kicking with your gate-side foot. Position him and keep him positioned with your outside leg. Keep your legs reliably on him so you keep his confidence, and aid unnoticeably. Aid rhythmically for fluid performance. These are the things that make the winning performance.

I set up an outside trail course for our Combined Training Event and Horse Show. It was a simple course with water in the creek bed, gate on the hillside, vine-hung trees, a bridge across a small, shallow gully, helter-skelter logs and brush and a 2-foot straight bank to hop up. There were both Combined Training horses and show trail horses entered.

Now Combined Training horses must be ridden in a dressage test and so should be on the aids. Show trail horses should at least be accustomed to simple obstacles. Right? Yet not one of those horses could be put through the entire course. Most balked at the water, many flipping this way and that and even whirling away. Not a single horse could be positioned to open the gate simply going through frontwards. The bridge gave as much trouble as the water and the Combined Training horses wanted to jump the logs. Who was riding whom?

Whether a horse walks or trots across a log or

Hilda Gurney judging. An excellent approach to the water hole: the horse is looking but going forward on the aids.

Another excellent approach to the water hole.

When the horse is not between your hands and legs, he can do pretty much as he pleases. This one did not like the water hole.

jumps it should be your option, not his. In the canter he will jump because canter bounds are jumping bounds. In the walk or trot all you have to do with a horse that is on the bit is simply continue forward in the rhythm of the stride on even contact. This tells the horse to continue walking or trotting as he crosses the log. If you want him to jump, all you have to do is use a half-halt on approach followed by a smooth push. Over he hops. There is no reason for being at the mercy of your horse's whims. The trained horse should be on your wave length, not giving you a lot of static.

Gymkhana provides lots of fun for lots of people and lots of mental and physical anguish for lots of horses. The Great American Horse and Rider Training Program has been "Do It Enough Times and You'll Learn How." As a result we have riders jerking horses around with the reins to try to control them and horses so soured by this and by constant, painful work on barrels, et al, that they often will not even go into the arena anymore.

If you are going to win in stiff competition of any sort, the principles of basic training are always the same because all horses basically have the same mental and physical characteristics. They are all horses! Our top barrel racers use and teach these basic principles and the American Horse Shows Association is working hard at putting horsemanship into gymkhana. Still we have lots of backlot experts who teach their misknowledge to myriads of home-club competitors and so the Great American Horse and Rider Training Program persists.

Everywhere I go I see barrels guarding the three points of the mystical triangle of the altar to the games god. Often there is the aisle of the poles leading to the triangle. The last things you need in training the gymkhana horse are the barrels and the poles. All basic training and ninety percent of the conditioning and specialized training should be done without them.

The training I have taken you through lays the foundation for all gymkhana maneuvers. All you must do from there on is gradually increase your horse's physical ability and mental understanding to respond quickly and smoothly. From the canter from the walk on designated lead, you develop the canter from the halt by pushing the horse onto the bit first and then asking for the canter on the lead you want. Use the proper aids for the lead and be satisfied with a nice, exact canter. From that you can gradually increase the balance and the length of the first bound until you have the leap into the gallop on designated lead.

In the same way gradually make the canter circles smaller and get the canter turn on the haunches until your horse is balanced enough and supple enough to make the turns needed for games. Do not ask for speed until the horse can do it well at the canter. Then gradually increase the speed of the turn by increasing the balance. Good stops come from balance, too; first from the walk, then from the trot, and then from the canter and gradually from more speed. Push the horse onto the bit with your legs as you lower your seat.

Flying changes of lead require balance and timing. When you ride the canter properly, you half-halt lightly each time his back takes your seat forward. If you half-halt stronger and then reverse your aids, the horse is balanced and your timing is right for the flying change. Build up to it by canter right a few yards, walk and canter left a few yards until the horse does it easily without excitement. Then it is time to patiently try the flying change. Speed comes later.

The changes of speed you already have—you only have to develop the horse's ability to change rapidly from extension to collection to extension. Any time a horse lengthens his stride to cover ground, he will go a lot faster than he would if he took a lot more shorter strides at a much faster rhythm. He will also slow down quicker and easier because he has not lost his balance in extending and his rhythm remains the same at every speed. This makes him highly maneuverable for games.

About twenty years ago I saw a barrel race in Paso Robles, California. All the competitors except one dashed and jerked through the pattern, many of them spurring or batting on the homestretch, causing the horses to visibly slow down each time the spurs or bat connected. But one competitor was an older man on a reined horse, obviously a pair in from the ranch in their Sunday best to have a little fun. Their ride was so smooth it looked as if they were out for a canter in the park. There was not a wasted motion anywhere—the horse and rider were a molded unit; and when the horse ran for the finish, he lengthened his stride so smoothly that you felt he was still cantering.

They tied with a girl and repeated the performance with the same ease and precision in the runoff for first place; but I was greatly disappointed. I will never know if they would have beaten the girl or not because the man pulled up just before crossing the finish line. Whether he knew the girl and did not want to risk beating her or just got momentarily confused, he lost to her by a fraction of a second.

Which brings me to words of advice on playing the games. Lay your foundation training well; gradually develop the ultimate performance; work on the contest pattern just enough to know each move to make and which things need refinement. Then in running the course avoid any excited moves, asking the horse smoothly and confidently for the positions, balance and speed you want at the moment. When you can ride this way on a trained horse that responds smoothly and readily, you will

"Finish an endurance ride with his head up" does not mean with head up and back down under an unbalanced rider. The second horse is not hanging his head. He is still traveling with relaxed, long strides under a relaxed rider who could get in still better balance by lowering his knees.

make fast time. When you just get out and ride as if the sheriff is after you, you will lose time, place and your happy horse.

One other area I would like to touch on is that of endurance riding. All the instructions in this that I have seen just deal with conditioning—how to feed, how much work in each gait, how much stress, how to take TPR's, equipment to prevent sore backs, shoeing practices, etc. It seems to me certain basic facts are ignored. For instance: if you supple both sides of your horse so he bends equally both ways, he will keep the saddle straight on his back and you will be able to ride in balance with him. These things prevent sores—horse and human. Teaching him to respond to all the turning aids gets

him bending properly. If he engages his hocks— that is, steps under his haunches and bends all those joints—he will negotiate all kinds of terrain more easily, carrying himself and you more easily. This lessens fatigue.

The exercises I have given you—leg yielding, turn on the haunches, transitions in gaits and in extension-collection—all increase engagement, balance and responsiveness. They help develop strength where it counts: in the haunches and the back.

If a horse will go fast by extending his stride rather than taking quicker, shorter steps, he will cover ground quicker with fewer strides per mile. This lessens the stress on feet and legs as well as on his muscles. If he readily changes from extension to collection, sudden changes in terrain can be negotiated easily without mental and physical stress on the horse. If the horse works on contact, you can help him over difficult spots by helping him balance. This certainly does not rule out loose rein work in places where he needs freedom to use his head as a balancing rod.

If a horse works relaxed with his head lowered and his back up and swinging, he can carry you on his back more easily. You do not tire so quickly because his gaits are smoother. Tired rider, tired horse. Relaxed muscles—both his and yours—do not load up with poisonous wastes that cause both fatigue and tying up.

I submit that a training-conditioning program based on this basic dressage would put your endurance horse in better condition with less time and miles because he would be working even on his rest days when he is longed only. He would be working when schooled in the arena and the schooling would help you help him over the rough country. When all these points I have mentioned are added together, it means a horse and rider could go over all kinds of ground farther and faster with less stress. Isn't that what it's all about?

14

REINING
THE STOCK HORSE

I have seen the California reined stock horses working on the ranches and learned how to rein them from Bert Allen, a vaquero who was a top reinsman with Miller & Lux. When I first started training horses professionally, I used the California hackamore method. I quickly learned that most people do not understand how to use the hackamore properly, so I went to the regular snaffle and used it similarly to the hackamore; that is, getting the horse to accept it without accepting contact. Then I got interested in dressage and especially in comparing its basic principles with the principles involved in reining the stock horse.

Both methods evolved from those used in the Mediterranean area, especially the Iberian peninsula. Both dressage trainers and early Californians sought the same responses from the horses and used identical training movements in most cases. But the Europeans went into the riding halls and arenas and to the snaffle while the Californians stayed out in the hills and kept the bosal.

Dressage was developed for training war horses back in the days when the cavalry was used against foot soldiers and other cavalry. The reined horse was developed for doing all the work required in handling cattle on the open range. The modern, specialized dressage horse is used for dressage competition and exhibition, while the modern version of the reined horse is seen mostly in our show rings.

Unfortunately, the real California reined stock horse is a thing of the past. The vaqueros were not men of letters. They had their cow work to do and their reined horses to use in doing it. With the horses there to show what they were talking about, they used simple phrases to describe the ideal performances. On top of this, they were quite secretive, passing on their training methods to only a select few. These simple vaquero phrases were written into the AHSA rule book as guidelines for the stock horse class. This worked fine until horse shows became such big business that the judges and exhibitors were no longer working ranchers and vaqueros, but professional trainers instead.

Soon "on a loose rein" was taken literally, whereas the true reined horse was worked on contact, going on a truly loose rein only from here to there. "Hind feet well under him" got to be so far forward that "after allowing the horse to gather itself" had to be added, since no horse is in a position to continue working when he stops with his hind feet under his elbows.

The sliding stop became a requirement rather than a by-product of the square stop in slick footing, this latter being one of the reasons for developing the square stop in the first place. The pivot became the spin, a movement of no value in working cattle; and the square stop and pivot in turning a cow has been displaced by the rollback—a dangerous practice in slick footing.

All of these things have come about gradually through the emergence of judges who were unfamiliar with the reined stock horse. The judges place the winners, who are copied by the rising trainers—and so the performance changes according to the judges' interpretations.

I tell you these things so you will understand that any comparisons I make between dressage horses and reined horses are with the real working stock horses, not the show-ring product of today. The last true reined horse I have seen was Sheila Varian's Ronteza. Sheila and Ronteza won highest honors at a time when judges were consistently giving the blues to flashy imitations. Quality cannot be denied all the time by all the judges.

The hackamore is an excellent training tool but quite misunderstood today. It does not lend itself to training in the arena, nor does make-work in the corral develop the very best stock horse. The biggest differences in the two methods, basic dressage and reining, come from the ways the snaffle and the hackamore must be used to get proper results. Keeping these things in mind and going through the following comparisons with me, see if you do not think it is logical to go to basic dressage to rein a horse when you are forced more and more out of the hills into the arena.

The dressage horse must do a canter pirouette without loss of canter strides and rhythm, touching his front feet to the ground six times in a complete turn. This would be impractical when working cattle, so the reined horse is expected to pivot a quarter turn or less in one "stride" with his inside hind foot grounded. That way he is in position to pivot back the other direction without hesitation if the cow ducks back. To be highly maneuverable in the pivots and pirouettes the horse must be very well collected. Anyone who has watched stock horse classes has seen horses start the pivot only to fall out to the front and have to heave—or be heaved—to finish the pivot.

If a horse is trained to be pushed onto the bit for collection, he can be balanced with a strong half-halt if the pivot starts to fall apart. If he has been developed with proper exercises so that all the joints of his hindquarters become supple, then he will bend all those joints in being collected, giving him better balance and making him less likely to fall forward. Putting him together for the pivot, then, is not a case of pulling him back onto the haunches, but rather of pushing him onto the bit. This does not cause him to step forward, but makes him sink in the rear as those joints bend, and so raise in front ready to pivot, step back or leap ahead as needed. This is how it was done by the vaqueros. This is how it is done in dressage.

While working a horse against a fence can get him turning obediently and shifting his weight toward the rear, only those horses naturally the most supple in their joints will learn to "squat" to make the turns. Those not-so-naturally supple will push their hind feet farther under and bend in the loin, giving a false feeling of collection. Since this bending of all the joints is a thing most stock horse trainers apparently are not aware of, present day stock horses are not bred for this suppleness; so the trainers more and more would have to "exercise" the horses into it.

Working on the fence gives the obedience and some shifting of the horse's weight, but too much of this work also sours the horse. With dressage exercises such as leg yielding on the circle, change through the circle, reverse half circles—all of them gradually done in smaller and smaller areas—the horse has a chance to loosen up and bend all those joints of his hindquarters.

The same is true of the stops. If you get a horse making a square, balanced halt from the walk, then the trot and then the canter all by driving him onto the bit, all this going along as you supple him more and more, then he learns to stop with his feet well under him where they belong—under the haunches. This is the dressage halt: balanced and square and sinking in the hindquarters. Fast stops from the gallop developed from this halt keep the

Kathy Hansen and Apache. Apache, schooled to third level in dressage, demonstrates his ability to perform as a stock horse in the pivot.

horse in position to pivot, back or leap out without your "allowing the horse to gather himself." Then you truly have a working cowhorse rather than an unreasonable facsimile thereof.

And so it is with backing. None of this scooting backward with jerks on the reins. The reined horse stepped firmly back on invisible rein aids, well balanced and ready to leap ahead or pivot in a split second. This is the dressage reinback. War work or cow work—a man's life and job depended on good working horses.

Flying changes are necessary in cow work because, as we all know, it is dangerous to make small circles on the wrong lead. The horse has difficulty balancing himself and finds it impossible to bend in the direction of the turn, making him

Kathy Hansen and Apache. Apache backs the way a working stock horse should,
calmly and under control.

quite awkward. Put a horse in a situation where he sees that he needs to change leads, and he will do it of his own accord—providing he is naturally capable of it and the rider has not interfered with his balance. But in dry work in the show ring the horse must change leads because he is asked to do it.

You should train the horse to make clean changes going straight. The practice of turning the horse out and suddenly in, hoping he will make the change, is impractical in working situations and dangerous at any time. I saw a hackamore colt fail to make the change this way so the rider again turned him out and quickly back. By then the colt was so strung out that he simply could not get his inside foreleg forward. It folded back under him and he fell, breaking the rider's leg.

I get static about aids—"I can't be bothered with all that stuff when I'm working a cow!" If you practice the proper combinations of aids during all your training and riding, it becomes reflex action just like the moves you make in driving a car. When you reach that point, you will not only use those aids for everything you do with the horse, you will automatically use them to correct his mistakes and so improve his total performance.

In working your cowhorse for showing, avoid putting him through the routine at any time. Some years back I watched the hackamore class at a show in Paso Robles, California. By reinsman standards, the only hackamore horse in the class was Sheila Varian's Ronteza; but the judge came up with a three-way tie for first. To break the tie, Sheila and the other two had to make the run and sliding stop followed by stepping back instead of the turn. Ronteza was the only horse that stepped back without hesitation. The other two fidgeted to the right and to the left before getting the message that they were to back. A reined horse should do anything you ask of him in any order you ask—not follow a pattern. After all, the cow does not follow any set pattern!

When a horse is fully trained in the snaffle, he will usually accept the hackamore, responding as well to it as he does to the snaffle. So when you are ready to put your horse straight up in the curb bit, you can easily make the transition by using the bosalillo, the lightweight bosal. The cheeks should be about three-eighths inch in diameter. A mane hair mecate about three-eighths inch in diameter should be used for reins. Mane hair is smoother and softer than tail hair, causing the horse and rider less discomfort. Hair is essential because it is resilient whereas mohair, cotton or nylon will simply stay tight, not giving the horse the relief which is as essential with the hackamore as softening the hands is with the snaffle. The bosalillo should be all rawhide to give it the correct amount of spring and weight.

To wrap the hackamore keep the bosalillo top side up—the way it goes on the horse's head—with the heel knot toward you. Now wrap it according to the following steps:

(1) Fold the tassel end of the mecate to make reins the right length to hook easily over the saddle horn when the horse's head is at rest.

(2) Pull these reins up between the cheeks of the bosalillo so they come out the top side.

(3) Take one wrap with the tassel end around only the right cheek.

(4) With the popper end of the mecate take one

The bosalillo with wraps ready to snug down.

wrap from the left side around both cheeks clockwise across the top of the bosalillo between the reins and the nosepiece.

(5) Subsequent wraps go across the top clockwise

145

behind the reins and the single wrap made by the tassel end.

(6) The final wrap goes between the cheeks at the heel knot so the popper end comes out the bottom beside the tassel.

Work the wraps down snug but not tight because you want the initial wrap to spring open on loose rein. This is one of the main reasons for wrapping this way. Other reasons are that the mecate forms a straight bar to contact the horse's jaw, the reins are closest to his jaw, and it is very easy to adjust the number of wraps. Simply pull the mecate up to loosen the final wrap to give you slack. Add or subtract the appropriate number of wraps and pull the end of the mecate out of them. Then adjust the wraps snug again.

You find the spot to hang the breaking and training hackamore on the horse's nose by pinching down the bridge of his nose until you hit the spot that makes him duck his head slightly. The bosalillo can be hung slightly higher than this and can be a little looser under the jaw, leaving about an inch of space instead of only the half-inch needed in training. So after you find the place to hang the bosalillo, adjust the number of wraps needed to get this spacing.

The curb bit selected should have a straight bar mouthpiece, with or without the roller port and spade, and should have only mild leverage. If it is a half-breed or spade, it should be loose-jawed—the cheeks hinged to the mouthpiece. Also, it is important that the part of the cheeks from the mouthpiece upward are bent out so there is room for the bosalillo between them and the horse's nose. It will fit right in the groove above his mouth when these parts are bent out some.

I prefer rein chains on the bit. The fully trained horse—both dressage and reined—leaves a slight droop in the reins when working balanced and on contact. Dressage work is precise and cadenced, but cow work comes and goes according to the cow. Rein chains give both the horse and rider the feel of

Apache, acquainted with the double bridle, readily accepts the properly adjusted spade bit and bosalillo.

contact at times when the reins must be loose to give the horse freedom to cover rough ground.

First get your horse used to wearing the curb bit by turning him daily, saddled and bridled, into a stall or small corral for about an hour. Tie the reins up so they are just barely loose when his head is at rest. The proper way to bridle a horse with a spade

Kathy Hansen and Apache. Initially the reins are adjusted so the light hackamore works alone, letting the horse just wear the bridle.

Apache yields to both the light hackamore and the bit. When he is working more in the bridle, the hackamore reins are held below the bridle reins.

bit is to hold the headstall the same as always but hold the bit by the near shank, insert the spade in the side of the horse's mouth and bring it down into position as he opens his mouth. Then lift it into his mouth by the headstall.

After the horse is used to wearing the curb, you can start riding him in the two reins. Since he is already trained and neckreining well, start out carrying both mecate reins together in one hand the way I have told you to hold the snaffle reins between your ring and little fingers. The curb reins come in under your little finger and out over the top of your knuckles under your thumb, letting the romal or ends of the reins hang down on the off side. Shorten your curb reins enough that the chains do not flop but leave them long enough in relation to the hackamore reins that you are not yet using the curb.

Put the horse through a program of exercises that follows the training program we have been going through. As you do this, gradually shorten the curb reins in relation to the hackamore reins. When any exercise or movement gives him difficulty with the curb, increase the use of the hackamore, getting him used to the curb gradually. When he is doing everything well with both the curb and the hackamore together, start carrying the hackamore reins below the curb reins so you can gradually lengthen them more and more. Leave the hackamore on him for a few weeks after you stop using it until you are absolutely sure it is no longer needed.

That about wraps up my thoughts on the relationship between basic dressage and reining the stock horse. For a horse to reach his peak in this speciality, he should have plenty of range riding and cow work. With modern range work centered more on riding lawn mowers and chlorinating "water holes", it's frustrating to try to find the necessary work and the room to roam. That's one reason basic dressage is so desperately needed—it's a workable substitute.

15

PREPARING FOR JUMPING

I want to show you the relation of this basic training to the training of a jumping horse and what special basics are needed for him. I do not claim to be an expert in this field, but I have closely monitored clinics by international instructors and have consulted with knowledgeable students of these clinics. What I pass on is what I have learned from these sources.

It does not take an expert to see the difference between well-schooled jumpers and the hit-and-miss type. It is exciting to watch a horse charge up to a fence, hold your breath waiting for a refusal or a mighty leap, and then involuntarily rare back in your seat to help slow the horse down enough for him to make the turn into the next fence. The sighs of relief when such a horse makes it through a course sound like a herd of cows blowing off when they bed down.

On the other hand, it's thrilling to watch a horse flow through a course, sailing over each fence, changing speed and balance to make the turns and never rushing into or off a fence like a scared jackrabbit. Any person who isn't an equine-oriented stuntman would certainly prefer the latter.

The former can be quite frustrating to the rider. Why does a horse rush into, refuse, pop over or rush away from a fence? Basically it can be lack of good seat and hands of the rider, lack of understanding of the horse's capabilities, or lack of control of the horse.

When a horse is bumped on his mouth and back at every fence, he soon tries to avoid the pain by refusing, or to run away from it by rushing. When he's put at a pole he can hardly see so that suddenly there's this 3-foot-high barrier in front of him, he must stop, pop over or go through. When his rider shifts to the forward position on approach, all weight is suddenly thrown forward and he has to rush to keep up with the change in balance. If you just take your horse over fences to see if he can learn how, how can you gain control when things happen so fast and frantically? God has more to look after than just fools and little children.

There are several goals to keep in mind as you put yourself and your horse through the basics of jump training. First is the seat you want to develop. Caprilli developed the forward seat to correct the instability of a rider's leaning back and shoving his feet ahead. This forward seat was never used in schooling the horse in his basic training in the arena, but only over fences. While the forward seat was a huge improvement over the old style of riding over fences, it has two major drawbacks: it weights the forehand of the horse when it is crucial for him to be able to rise to the fence, and it makes the rider's back and legs largely ineffective, causing loss of control.

Stiff international competition not only brought about improvements but proved them to be winning improvements. This is what has developed and what you should keep in mind as you build your ability—and your horse's—in fencing. Shorten your irons two to four holes for cavalletti and fence work and for cross country trotting and galloping. Never use a stock saddle for jumping—it is dangerous. In riding with the shortened irons, maintain your basic position, keeping your knees lowered and your heels in a line directly under your hips. You should land down into your knees over fences—not knees that are clamped onto the saddle but knees that point down toward the ground, tightening the fork of your legs onto the wedge of the horse's back.

Always look ahead, never down at the cavalletti or fence. The horse will either clear the fence or he will not, but certainly he does not need his balance upset by your looking down. Approach sitting upright so you can use your seat to tell the horse "definitely forward." Stay upright over canter cavalletti and the horse will raise his forehand and hindquarters alternately under you. At fences stay upright; and as the horse rises to the fence, you are still upright to the ground but in a forward position in relation to the horse. Stay in this position in relation to him until his neck starts up on landing and he puts you back upright.

It is important that you get this rhythm and that you learn to maintain contact with the horse's mouth all the way, but you cannot learn both at once. A neckstrap—an old stirrup leather is good—buckled so it stays about in the center of the horse's neck where you can grab it easily is a big help, or you can grab his mane there. To do this you have to drop contact, so be sure to do it one stride before the fence since dropping contact right at the fence can cause a horse to fall. After you have developed seat and rhythm for jumping, you can learn to maintain contact.

I used to jump Pi Dough over logs out in the woods. Being the cowardly type and knowing that it is never right to learn a thing by just doing it, I started by first walking and later trotting him up to small logs about a foot thick. On approach I took a handful of mane; and as he lifted to hop over, I bent my elbows—a natural reaction to maintain the same feel of the hold. As he "jumped," this pulled me forward with him; and as he landed with his front legs, my hold relaxed letting everything level out again. While this was actually the feel of a canter cavalletti, it taught me the feel of the rhythm and made it possible for me to go on in rhythm to greater heights.

You can do the same with a canter cavalletti at the 16-inch height. If your seat, hands and balance need improving, do it before starting canter cavalletti work. Then as you go through a graduated training program, you and the horse can develop together instead of practice perfecting mistakes you would make trying to train the horse before you are capable of riding him.

As for contact, the horse shortens his frame on approach, lengthens it over the fence and shortens it again as his hind feet come forward in landing. Your elbows must close, open and again close in order for you to maintain contact. In order to do this, you have to have a secure seat. Work on it.

There are ideals you should keep in mind for your horse, too. Perhaps the most essential is rhythm. Your rhythm and balance and his are interdependent. If a horse is to flow through a jump course, he must maintain the same rhythm throughout, shortening his stride but not quickening his rhythm to make the short turns between fences, lengthening his stride when needed on approach. Remember that speed is not needed to take a fence—just rhythm and balance. To develop control of your horse's rhythm, balance and length of strides, you must work him on the flat in the basics I have given you.

Another essential for effective jumping is that the horse arc over the fence. If the horse throws his head up and his back down, his hindquarters are out behind him where he cannot use them to push over the fence. If he comes into a fence this way, he will have to leap higher to get his feet over and his landing will be dangerous to both of you. The basic

schooling on the flat—lowering the horse's head and getting him to stride under—develops the horse's ability to arch his back. Graduated cavalletti and fence work confirms this ability.

Let us look at the things a horse must be able to do to be a good jumper. He has to carry you through the course; and to carry you, he must be able to carry himself. To carry himself he must travel in proper position: with lowered head, yielded to the bit and striding under—raising his whole forehand to balance back. He must be willing to go forward under control, relaxed, rhythmical, balanced and straight. Jumping calls for constant shifting of balance, lateral bend for sharp turns, engagement of the hocks for taking the fences, and changes of speed which can be done smoothly only through change of length of stride.

All of these things are essential for consistently good jumping. How could you possibly teach them to your horse by just putting him at fences? These are the things we have been teaching the horse in his flat work. So you can see that the only logical way to have that winning jumper, hunter or Combined Training horse is to be thorough in his basic training.

But you do not have to complete this training before starting the basic training for jumping. When your horse is at least five years old and far enough along to trot and canter with long, relaxed, rhythmic strides yielded to the bit, it is time to start. Start with the trot cavalletti, getting him to take them with relaxed rhythm.

When he is doing this well, set up a pair of standards eight feet beyond the last cavalletto. This gives the horse what is called one empty stride before reaching the standards—that is, he trots one stride that is not over a pole. Lay a pole on the ground between the standards. This is to get him used to the pole being there, not to get him to jump over it. After two or three times of trotting through this setup, place two poles on the standards to form an X in the middle, one end of each pole on each

Details of the X fence set twenty feet beyond the last cavalletto.

standard at about two-and-one-half to three feet height and the other ends on the ground beside the standards. Place a single pole on the ground next to the standards on the approach side.

Trot through this sitting up straight and maintaining rhythm. As the horse bounds over the X, he will change to the canter. Push him smoothly but firmly down to the trot and continue on around the arena to take the whole thing again. Do this four or five times without stopping so the horse develops a definite rhythm.

When this work is going well, introduce your horse to the canter cavalletti. These are three poles set at about 20-inch height and ten feet apart. If you made the box ends for your cavalletti, turn them to the highest setting and measure from pole to pole for the ten feet. You can start at the intermediate height but this can cause the horse to try to trot through them. If you have trouble, it is better to start him on just one and add another and then the third one as his confidence and yours build up. Also, it is best to wrap your horse's legs for cavalletti and fence work so they do not get banged up if he makes a misstep.

Approach the canter cavalletti at a trot. As the horse bounds over the first one, he will then be in the canter. Sit up straight and maintain contact. Look straight ahead and tell him "definitely forward." If he rushes into them, make sure you are not speeding up your trot rhythm or leaning forward and

Kathy Hansen and Watirah. Approaching the first canter cavalletto, Watirah has anticipated and changed to the canter. Note the neck strap.

The horse's form is good. The rider has rounded her back. When keeping your hands on the horse's neck, bend forward from the hips.

Headed for the one empty stride before the X fence. Very nice form.

Kathy Hansen and Watirah. Watirah's hind feet go into the track of her front foot as she prepares to take the fence. Kathy demonstrates how leaning forward weights the horse's forehand.

Kathy Hansen and Watirah. Make use of natural obstacles and the arena training when riding out. With the rider's seat out of the saddle, Watirah can (and did previously) refuse the log.

upsetting his balance. If he rushes out of them, make sure you are not bumping his mouth or upsetting his balance. Bring your horse firmly to a trot five or six strides beyond the cavalletti, trot on around to take them again, doing this four or five times before stopping in order to develop confidence and rhythm.

When this is going well, you can put a fence twenty feet beyond the last canter pole. This gives the horse one empty canter stride before the fence. Start with the X fence and gradually advance the horse to more height. It is best to use two or more poles at staggered heights, placing the lower one first and the next higher one about a foot beyond at the 20-foot mark. Then a third one can be a foot beyond that and a little higher. If the horse begins

rushing off the fence, place another cavalletto twenty feet beyond the fence. The horse will usually look forward to that and you can maintain your seat over it, going smoothly onto a circle after it to control the rhythm of the canter.

As the horse advances in ability and confidence, place a single fence on the other side of the arena so you can canter on around and take it. It should look solid, and bales of straw are handy for this. From here on you can introduce him to a variety of fences set at different places, always working for rhythm and calmness. A horse can jump at least four-and-one-half feet at a smooth hand gallop, so do not ever feel that you must rush him at a fence to gain momentum to get over.

Jumping is strenuous work that can cripple a

With proper schooling applied in the cross country, time-wasting refusals can be avoided. This rider is handling the situation well.

horse that is not in condition for it. Therefore you should have a definite training and conditioning program. On the horse's day of rest he should be longed for half an hour. Initially in his training he should be longed before going into each session of arena work. As his training progresses, this can be discontinued. When he is under control, he should be ridden out once a week; and when the cavalletti work starts, he should be warmed up with flat work before going over the cavalletti. One day a week is sufficient for cavalletti work at the start.

As the horse's basic schooling progresses, you will want to add a second day of riding out and then a second day of cavalletti-fence work. Finally you can do some light fence work on the schooling days too, and always warm up with schooling on the two days of concentrated fence work. So eventually your program would go something like this: rest day with light longeing; basic schooling day with light fencing; cavalletti day and/or fencing day; riding out

day; and then a repetition of the second, third and fourth days which takes you to the rest day again.

In riding out use all the schooling your horse has at that time. Gradually build up his physical fitness and ability to negotiate uneven terrain. When he is taking easy fences in the arena, take easy, natural obstacles outside. Never, in any work, tire your horse so much that he gets disgusted, but do "stress" him just a little in order to build him up. I realize this is a very ambiguous instruction, but no two horses are alike in physical and mental ability so no one can tell you to do ten minutes of this work or fifteen minutes of that. You have to feel it out for your horse.

All work of any kind should end with a free walk on loose rein, although there are times when I jump off, loosen the girth and stop all work because the horse has accomplished something that has been especially difficult for him. That is a reward he really appreciates!

Rider sitting down on the horse and looking ahead to the next part of the L fence. The horse is on the aids and arcing over beautifully.

Across the first part of this same L fence, the horse has landed out of balance and the rider compounds the problem by pulling the horse around. Basic schooling could help eliminate such situations.

With the horse schooled properly, this rider could sit down and drive the horse onto the bit to collect him for this short turn in the stadium jumping.

When you can lengthen your horse's strides and balance him easily toward the rear, you can start positioning him at fences. Where his front feet land in a gallop is where his hind feet will land for take-off. *Make use of your schooling work in all fence work. Do not switch to stop-and-go driving just because there are a few fences to leap over.*

When you can collect your horse easily, you can start taking the turns needed before and after fences to prepare the horse for stadium and cross-country jumping. Work into them gradually—do not expect him to make short turns easily all in one day. Flying changes usually are not any problem if you always look ahead in the direction you will go next since the easiest place for the horse to change is when he is airborne over a fence. If he must change leads on course, get it through the trot until he has been schooled in flying changes.

I love to watch jumpers in any category when they take the course so smoothly that it looks effortless. Those that are dashed up to a fence, spurred over, hauled down in speed and cranked around the turns just excite my sympathy.

16

RIDING THE DRESSAGE TEST

There is really no comparison between show classes and dressage classes. In a show you go round and round with ten to twenty other riders, hoping the judge will see and remember the good things your horse does. You get a ribbon or you do not, but in either case, you often wonder why. Different judges interpret the standards in different ways, leaving you wondering just how you should train your horse to win.

Dressage tests are about as fair as any that can be devised. The way a horse should perform at each given level is pretty thoroughly defined and understood; and recognized judges, graded according to the levels they may judge, must attend a judges' forum every other year to maintain their standings. An international judge presides at the forum; all judges judge actual rides, and all of them must have reasons for their scoring. "I like the horse" or "it was a good ride" is not a valid reason. They have to get into the fine points of how the horse moves, how relaxed he is, how he does transitions and so on. Since all this is written down during judging, little is left to memory. The process eliminates a lot of guess work on the part of the judges.

The tests, which are rewritten about every three years, are designated by levels: Training, 1st Level through 4th Level, and international competition levels of Prix St. George, Intermediare, and Grand Prix. All levels are graduated, starting with the basics and advancing with the systematic training of the horse. Within each level are usually two different tests, Test 2 being more advanced than Test 1. So the tests not only make it possible for you to show your horse as his training starts and develops, but also to let you learn in what order it should develop.

At a show you are allowed to ride all the tests in any two consecutive levels—Training and 1st Levels, 1st and 2nd Levels, etc.—but not Training and 2nd, 1st and 3rd, and so on. While it is a good idea to ride two tests in a day so the first one can serve as a warm-up, it is not so good to ride more than that because a tired horse and rider cannot turn in as good a performance. The horses are judged according to the level. For example, the working trot and canter are not expected to be as well developed in Training Level as in 1st Level, so they are judged accordingly. This means that the higher the level, the more exacting the demands of the judge.

The neat thing about riding in a dressage show is that you have the judge's undivided attention for the three to eight minutes it takes to ride the test. While you ride, he observes the performance and dictates the score and any appropriate comments for each movement to the writer sitting beside him. The writer records these scores and comments on a copy of the test—this same copy to be turned over to you at the end of the class. This gives you what amounts to a private lesson which often includes person-to-person suggestions at the end of your ride.

Often you can ride for some of the best dressage instructors in the country, and that is a lot for your money.

Take a look at this training level dressage test. On the back you are told the purpose and conditions of the test, the meanings of the scores and the cost of the error of getting off-course. At much higher levels a transition three or more strides off the designated point may be considered off-course. The premium list of the show should tell you if you are to ride in the large arena instead of the small one. On the front are spaces for information for the judge's writer, the show secretary and you. The diagrams of the small and large arenas are there so you do not have to seek the information elsewhere.

There is no available reason for the choice of letters, so do not ask; but the purpose is to name definite points on the track and the centerline to make it possible to tell you and the judge the starting point of each movement to be performed. Looking inside at the test itself, we find some of these letters listed in the left-hand column. Opposite each letter or combination of letters is the instruction for the movement that should begin at that point. The next column tells what the judge is looking for and what you are trying to achieve.

Now let us ride this test so you will know how to translate one from paper to the arena and how to make a good ride while you are about it. First of all you need to know when and how you get into that inner sanctum—the dressage court.

Dressage rides are all scheduled in advance and you are notified before coming to the show of the exact riding time of each test you are riding. It is your responsibility to be there ready to enter the arena at the time. You cannot be required to ride before that time, although at some shows if there are several unfilled scratches you may be asked if you are willing to. If you do not want to ride sooner for any reason, you have the right to say "no."

There is a warm-up area where you can prepare your horse for the ride. After the rider before you

TRAINING LEVEL TEST 1

REQUIREMENTS:
20m circles in trot and canter

INSTRUCTIONS:
Transitions into and out of the halt
may be made through the walk

NO.

		TEST	DIRECTIVE IDEAS	POINTS	COEFFICIENT	TOTAL	REMARKS
1.	A X	Enter working trot sitting Halt, salute, proceed working trot sitting	Straightness on center line, transitions, quality of halt and trot				
2.	C H E K	Track left Working trot rising Circle left 20m Working trot sitting	Quality of turn at C, quality of trot, roundness of circle				
3.	Between K&A	Working canter left lead	Calmness and smoothness of depart				
4.	A	Circle left 20m	Quality of canter, roundness of circle				
5.	Between B&M	Working trot rising	Balance during transition				
6.	HXF	Working walk	Straightness, quality of walk		x2		
7.	F	Working trot rising	Smoothness of transition				
8.	E H	Circle right 20m Working trot sitting	Quality of trot, roundness of circle				
9.	Between H&C	Working canter right lead	Calmness and smoothness of depart				
10.	C	Circle right 20m	Quality of canter, roundness of circle				
11.	Between B&F	Working trot sitting	Balance during transition				
12.	A X	Down center line Halt, salute	Straightness on center line, quality of trot and halt				

Leave arena at free walk on long rein at A

COLLECTIVE MARKS:

Gaits (freedom and regularity)			2		
Impulsion (desire to move forward, elasticity of the steps, relaxation of the back)			2		
Submission (attention and confidence; harmony, lightness and ease of movements; acceptance of the bit)			2		
Rider's position and seat; correctness and effect of the aids			2		

FURTHER REMARKS:

SUBTOTAL _____

ERRORS (–_____)

TOTAL POINTS _____

AMERICAN HORSE SHOWS ASSOCIATION
220 East 42nd Street
New York, NY 10017

1991
TRAINING LEVEL TEST 1

PURPOSE: To confirm that the horse has received proper dressage training as a result of which its muscles are supple and loose, it moves freely forward in clear and steady rhythm, accepting the bit. *(Drawing of arena shows movement #2.)*

CONDITIONS
Arena: Standard or small

Average Time:
˜ 5:00 standard arena
4:00 small arena

MAXIMUM POSSIBLE POINTS:
210

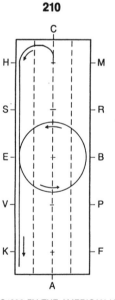

_____
Name of Competition

_____
Date of Competition

_____
Number and Name of Horse

_____
Name of Rider

FINAL SCORE

_____   _____
Points   Percent

_____
Name of Judge

_____
Signature of Judge

PURPOSE

To introduce the rider and horse to the basic
principles of dressage competition.

CONDITIONS

1. To be ridden in a plain snaffle with a noseband.

2. Arena size: 20m x 40m or 20m x 60m.

3. No time limit.

SCORING:

10 Excellent	5 Sufficient
9 Very Good	4 Insufficient
8 Good	3 Fairly Bad
7 Fairly Good	2 Bad
6 Satisfactory	1 Very Bad

0 Not Performed or Fall of Horse or Rider

PENALTIES: Errors: 1st error, 2 points; 2nd error, 4 points,
3rd error, elimination; leaving the arena,
elimination (When test is part of a combined
event, 3rd error, 8 points; 4th error, elimination)

APRIL 1, 1977

Betty Bevan and Shemali. Halt at X and salute. When first entering dressage tests, it's common for the horse to waver on the center line, halt unsquare and keep its attention on the judge's stand.

has started the free walk at the end of his ride, you are permitted to ride your horse around the outside of the dressage court, going past the judge's stand if you like. You are never allowed to ride in the dressage court at a show except during your actual rides. When the judge is ready for you to enter, he will ring his bell. You then have one minute to enter the arena. Even if you happen to be right at the judge's stand, this gives you plenty of time to trot your horse to the other end, make a circle or two outside and get lined up trotting straight in at A.

Failure to enter by the time your minute is up means elimination. Other reasons for elimination are carrying the whip, the horse stepping all four feet out of the arena, and leaving the arena at any place other than A. You won't even be allowed to come in if your bit has a rough mouthpiece or you have side reins, draw reins or a martingale on the horse.

The judge sits a few feet beyond C looking straight down the centerline so he can see if you can keep your horse on the straight and narrow. Start the trot outside and look straight ahead at the judge's stand as you enter at A sitting. Push your horse onto the bit, riding by feel and driving more with your right side if the horse veers to the left (and vice versa). Just do not correct him with the reins because that would cause over-steering and a very wobbly centerline.

Two or three strides before X, push into a nice transition to the walk and then the halt at X (halt through the walk). If it is a crooked halt, do not try to correct it. Believe me, it happens at top-most levels and trying to correct it only causes more problems plus confusing the horse's understanding that he should stand immobile when halted. To salute, take both reins in your left hand; let your right hand hang by your side and nod your head (a man re-

Betty Bevan and Shemali. A very nice trot circle with the horse properly bent for the large arc.

moves his hat). You do not continue the ride until the judge salutes you by rising and nodding.

After his salute, take the right rein back in your right hand and prepare your horse for going forward. You cannot take forever to prepare him, but it is fatal to feel as if you must hurry to go through the test. So take a brief moment to feel that you and the horse are ready to proceed, then walk a stride to go into the sitting trot and prepare to turn right onto the track at C. At M you start posting (rising). Your next instruction is at C; and since teleportation is not one of the accepted dressage gaits, you continue on around the track until your shoulder is even with C where you start sitting the trot. If the horse carries his forehand too close to the "fence" as you go down the track, drive with your inside leg to straighten him. At the same time keep your eyes ahead so you can prepare him for each corner and transition coming up.

Besides sitting the trot at C, you also start a circle. A circle must be round and this one is the width of the arena, so do not ride a corner toward M. Instead aim for a point on the track beyond M where you just touch the track as you continue on the circle. In the small arena the next point you touch would be X, but in the large arena it will not be so far out in the middle. The best way is to learn to ride circles by keeping your horse bent the right amount for the size of circle, but it is not easy. After touching the track before H, prepare to canter your horse at C.

The canter should start as your shoulder is even with C, but absolute precision is not quite as important as smoothness. It is better to be half a stride late than a stride early since the latter could be interpreted as anticipation on the part of your horse. To judge when to start preparation for the canter—or anything else—you must know your horse. If the

Coming off the circle at C to canter the corner, the horse has momentarily lost her balance and come above the bit.

horse takes the wrong lead, bring him smoothly back to the trot and keep him bent to get the proper lead. If you do not correct this you will probably get a zero for movement not performed.

Once again you circle the width of the arena, staying in the canter. Your next instruction is working trot (rising) at A. So you make the one canter circle, *go on the track at* C, canter through the corner, down the track, through the next corner to start the posting trot at A. If you do not mentally start riding the track at C after that canter circle, you will find yourself riding another quarter circle before reaching the track. This is poor performance.

The next thing happens at M, so on around the track you go, starting a change of rein at M that takes you through X, posting all the way through K and on to C, where you are told to start sitting the trot and go on a circle. In the change of hand, you continue on the arc of your corner, which means you will be a little beyond M when you are finally headed straight through X to a point on the track a little ahead of K. This allows you to make a smooth turn that touches at K and continues on around that corner.

Notice that in taking the sitting trot at A and making the trot circle followed by the canter circle

166

Carolyn Carroll and Ibn Jo Kar. A beautiful picture of impulsion and collection in the canter in a higher level. Spurring probably caused the flip of the horse's tail.

A winning higher level house caught in a bad moment. It happens to the best riders and horses, so do not worry that you might not be perfect.

Don Mackay and Saltation. A very nice final halt and salute at G in a higher level test. The horse's hind feet should be even too.

at A, you are doing a mirror image of the movements that started at C before. Upon reaching C in the canter, change to the sitting trot, going on down the track, planning ahead to make the turns short enough that you turn onto the centerline at A. If you waited until your shoulder is at A to make the turn, you would go beyond the line and have to come back to it. If you plan to continue the arc of your turn with your training level horse, you will come out pretty well to go straight onto the centerline.

Again, the halt through the walk and the salute. After the judge salutes you, ride forward in the walk, letting the horse chew the reins out of your hands. At most smaller shows where time permits,

the judge often talks to the rider after a ride. So look at the judge as you ride the free walk (loose rein) toward C to see if he is getting up to meet you. Whether he talks with you or not, finish your ride on a loose rein on the track. It is advisable to ride on the track nearest the audience. That way, if the horse spooks it will probably be toward the center rather than the outside to elimination. It is also advisable to ride just a little past A and make a small circle into the arena before exiting. That way, should the steward ever forget to close the gate during your ride, your horse will not be in the habit of ducking out as he approaches A.

You have no doubt noticed the horizontal lines through the test. These divide the movements; and the score and any comments between two lines belong to that movement. Usual scores for most of us are 4 and 5 with a sprinkling of 3 and 6. Judges are very stingy with 10, but with two thinking creatures going through the test together, who is going to be perfect! The judge's comments are usually more critical than complimentary—not because he wants to pick the ride to pieces but because it shows where you need more work. Sometimes his comments will tell you how to improve things.

Under collective marks, the judge emphasizes what he has seen in the test: whether or not the horse's gaits are rhythmical and relaxed; whether the horse goes forward willingly or has been restrained so much that he is afraid to go forward; whether or not the contact is reliable; whether or not the horse shows tension in transitions; and what the rider needs in order to correct his seat and aids. This last comment is especially important because how you ride directly affects the performance of the horse.

In scoring, your points are totaled and your errors subtracted. Talking to your horse, while not an error, is a fault—two points off each time the judge hears or sees you do it. Then your final score is converted to a percentage of the total possible points. The percentages determine the winners, but ties are broken by the total points in collective marks. Fifty to fifty-five percent is the average good ride. If you are rather consistently getting in the sixties, you should be ready to start the next higher level.

Even though the tests are divided into movements, you should not think of them that way. It is not one movement completed, draw a line, do another movement. The test should flow as if it were a complete song, not a few bars of this one and a few bars of that one. You have the introduction and a pause, then one mood flowing into another and another until you come down the centerline to the finale, and after the finale the exit to applause (hopefully).

There has never been a perfect ride and never will be. Once you understand dressage rides and what to look for in the performance and then get a chance to see international level rides, you realize that the world's top riders can miss the centerline, halt crooked, get jerky movements out of the horse and so on. Do not let it discourage you into thinking it is an impossible goal. Instead let it help you erase each mistake from your memory during a ride so you can concentrate on trying your best on the thing you are into at the moment.

You are probably thinking there is lots to think about: where to go next, aids for corners and transitions, how to keep your horse straight and on the bit, ad infinitum. If you have to do all these things mechanically, you will never make it; but during all your work in training yourself and your horse, you should be developing both feel and reflex action—feel for whether the horse is moving correctly and reflex action to correct it when he is not. You do not have to wait for perfection in these things in order to show; you just have to know what you're aiming for.

While learning the test, you can develop more feel and better reflexes. Seldom ride the test in practice, except just enough to get the feel of it and to see what parts need more work. If you ride the test again and again, the horse can get quite bored with the whole thing; learn what comes next and try to take you through it instead of doing what you tell him to do. Instead of riding it, mark out a miniature court and walk through the test until it becomes a part of you. It is just like learning the route through town to a new market—you might need the street signs at first, but after awhile you probably cannot even remember the names of the streets. And remember that all tests are in smoothly rideable order. You will not make an abrupt change of hand out of the wrong corner any more than you would plan on going to the market the wrong way on a one-way street.

So how does this develop your feel and reflexes?

As you go through the test on foot, imagine yourself riding it—how your horse should feel, what aids to use and how your horse should respond to them. After learning the route, ride it in your imagination again and again while having coffee, before going to sleep, etc. You will find that you have better feel of your horse when riding, that you apply the aids more correctly and that you have programmed your computer to take you through the test without your having to think where you should go next.

If you are afraid that you might blank out during the test, you are allowed to have a reader up through 4th Level. The reader stands at E or B and reads the test as you ride it. There are certain rules. He must read the test as written. That means he cannot coach from the sidelines, but it is permissible to omit a lot. For example, I just call "A, trot rising" in lower level tests since working trot is the only kind; "C circle" because the rider should know it is the width of the arena. "M change rein" because it is across the diagonal. But these things are between the reader and the rider.

The reader can read each instruction only once, therefore he should time it after the rider is committed to the movement he is in but soon enough that the rider can prepare for the one he is reading. Practice reading to yourself while the test is being ridden. That way you get the feel of changes that happen quickly so you must read more quickly, and those that take more time so you must wait to read the next instruction.

Read loudly and clearly. Be sure to enunciate the letters clearly. If the rider is momentarily confused, he will look for the letter to come up en route. If a rider gets off-course, the reader must not say a word to try to help him. The judge will ring his bell and the rider should immediately approach the judges' stand for instruction.

So there you have it. It is not nearly as complicated as it may sound. It just takes a little practice, and a good place to get that is at schooling shows. If you think it would psych you out to be out there alone with your horse in front of the judge and everybody, don't worry about it. A good friend of mine felt that way about it until she had a chance to try riding a test in my college class. At the end of the test she said, "You know, I was so busy riding that test I didn't remember there was ANYBODY watching me!" Go ahead and enter at A. But beware, it stands for Addiction!

INDEX

See also Table of Contents

S

T

W

Y